D1571571

SIMON &
SCHUSTER
CANADA

Simon & Schuster Canada
A Division of Simon & Schuster, Inc.
166 King Street East, Suite 300
Toronto, Ontario M5A 1J3

This Simon & Schuster Canada edition April 2021

SIMON & SCHUSTER CANADA and colophon are trademarks of Simon & Schuster, Inc.

For information about special discounts for bulk purchases, please contact Simon & Schuster Special Sales
at 1-800-268-3216 or CustomerService@simonandschuster.ca.

Manufactured in the United States of America

10 9 8 7 6 5 4 3 2 1

Library and Archives Canada Cataloguing in Publication

Title: Colour + neutral / Sarah Richardson.
Other titles: Colour and neutral | Collected. 3, Colour + neutral
Names: Richardson, Sarah, 1971– author.
Description: Simon & Schuster Canada edition. | Series statement: Collected ; 3
Identifiers: Canadiana (print) 20200342819 | Canadiana (ebook) 20200342835 | ISBN 9781982167073 (softcover)
| ISBN 9781982167097 (ebook)
Subjects: LCSH: Color in interior decoration. | LCSH: Interior decoration.
Classification: LCC NK2115.5.C6 R53 2021 | DDC 747/.94—dc23

ISBN 978-1-9821-6707-3
ISBN 978-1-9821-6709-7 (ebook)

Editorial Director Beth Hitchcock
Art Director Rose Pereira
Media Manager Jennifer Gibeau
Cover Photography Valerie Wilcox

Collected

BY SARAH RICHARDSON

VOLUME N° 3

Colour + Neutral

PUBLISHED BY SIMON & SCHUSTER
NEW YORK · LONDON · TORONTO · SYDNEY · NEW DELHI

Contents

PHOTOGRAPHY BY READ McKENDREE

I'LL ADMIT, I'M CURIOUS: What's your palette? Do you dive into colour, surrounding yourself with rich jewel tones or pretty pastels? Or are you content to thrive in calming, white-walled rooms? It's no secret that I'm a devotee of smoky blues and greens, but I can also get behind a soft scheme of oyster, cream, and grey, depending on the day. So believe me, I get it—selecting which route is right for your home can be hard. That's why we devoted the third volume of **Collected** to this very theme, and filled the pages with inspiring projects and super-smart designer insights that satisfy both sides of the colour/neutral equation. Now that home has become more important than ever, I hope you'll find all the ingredients you need to build your perfect, right-for-you palette. Happy decorating!

Sarah

WHAT'S YOUR COLOUR COMFORT FACTOR?

Our third issue addresses the dance between timeless, easygoing neutrals and colourful commitments that bring the energy. So we asked our contributors: Which way do you lean?

EDITORIAL TEAM

SRD TEAM

My inspiration files for my next house are full of dark, daring rooms and an abundance of wallpaper. For now, I'm sticking with white walls and colour injections via artwork, my prized pink vintage Persian rug, and more velvet pillows than I can count.

BETH HITCHCOCK
Editorial Director

Give me a room of clean white walls, pale wood floors, and cool grey furniture any day. It creates the most calming atmosphere when you're otherwise surrounded by the intense primary colours that come with the inevitable bins of toddler toys!

ROSE PEREIRA
Art Director

I'm about 70% neutral for a timeless, cohesive overall palette, and 30% colour for visual interest and conversational kick-starters like, "Where'd you get that?"

JENNIFER GIBEAU
Media Manager,
Sarah Richardson Design

Colourful rooms make me happy and more at ease. My home is my testing ground, and I like to use colours commonly found in nature—it allows for more saturation and feels more familiar. Often, I'll use subtle versions of the same colour for the bones of the room: the walls may be one colour, while I take the trim a shade or two darker or lighter.

MEREDITH ELLIS
Designer, "Southern Charm"

Colour is all about light. In open spaces, I use timeless neutrals and pale hues to create ethereal backdrops. Colour enters through art, sculptural furnishings, or as a way to define architecture. In private spaces, like a bedroom or library, I employ richer colours as neutrals by using them abundantly.

LISA THARP
Designer, "Classic on the Cape"

I like kitchens and bathrooms to be crisp and clean, but other living spaces really need the warmth of colour and I'm not afraid to use it full force and supplement with neutrals as small accents here and there.

CHAUNCEY BOOTHBY
Designer, "Beachhouse Blues"

I don't differentiate between something being a colour and something being a neutral; I am always looking to achieve the right balance. I adore saturated colours and use those to anchor the space, then I might add ivory or a hit of linen to create contrast.

GILLIAN GILLIES
Designer, "Colour Theory"

I've always been a white-wall person, but I recently took a risk and painted my main floor Honey Harbour (CC-170) by Benjamin Moore. It's a pale yellow that reflects the natural sunlight really well.

VIRGINIA MACDONALD
Photographer, "Colour Theory"

I live with a lot of white walls but collect items with more warmth. I'm drawn to art and objects that look like they were left out in the elements for a few years! My favourite palette is when I look out our windows into the woods, with its changing light and colours.

READ McKENDREE
Photographer, "Southern Charm,"
"Beachhouse Blues," "Classic on the Cape,"
and "Tudor Twist"

My space is about 90% neutral, and I wish I were brave enough to venture past mustard yellow. I do love to collect colourful abstract paintings and photographs, which really sing on white walls.

VALERIE WILCOX
Photographer, "Next Chapter Chic,"
"Retro Revival," and "Alpine Farmhouse"

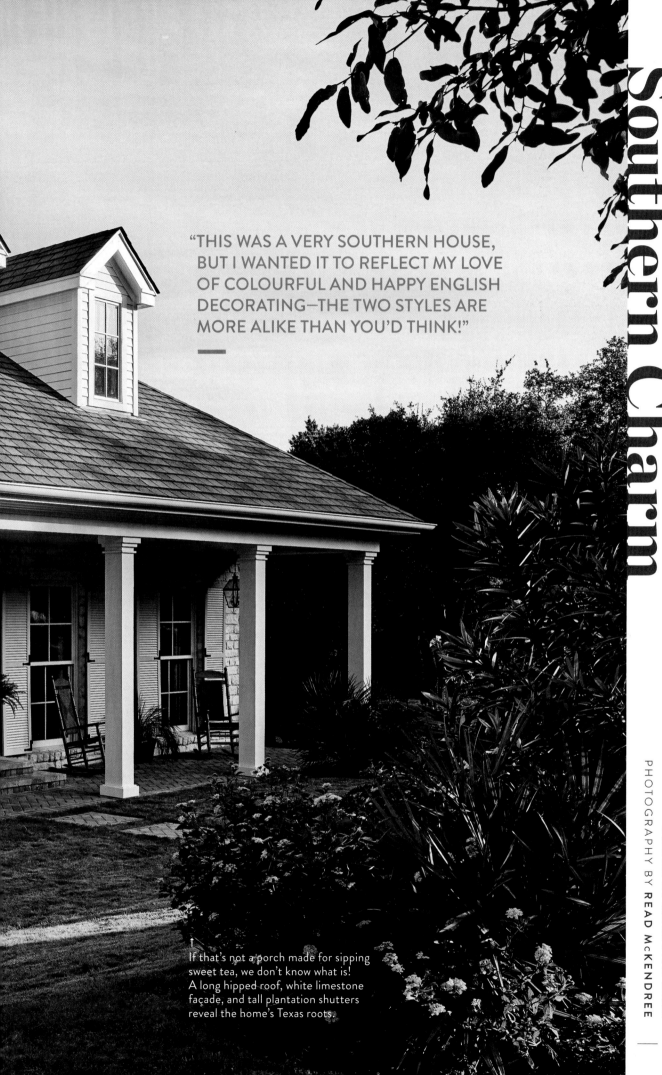

Southern Charm

"THIS WAS A VERY SOUTHERN HOUSE, BUT I WANTED IT TO REFLECT MY LOVE OF COLOURFUL AND HAPPY ENGLISH DECORATING—THE TWO STYLES ARE MORE ALIKE THAN YOU'D THINK!"
—

DESIGN BY **MEREDITH ELLIS**
PHOTOGRAPHY BY **READ McKENDREE**

If that's not a porch made for sipping sweet tea, we don't know what is! A long hipped roof, white limestone façade, and tall plantation shutters reveal the home's Texas roots.

DESIGN BY **MEREDITH ELLIS**, MEREDITH ELLIS DESIGN	AUSTIN, TEXAS	4.5 BATHROOMS	3 DORMER WINDOWS
	3,500 SQUARE FEET	4-MONTH RENOVATION	600 YARDS OF FABRIC
	4 BEDROOMS	1 IMAGINARY CLIENT	

S OME HOUSES HUM softly, others sing out loud—and it's no mystery which category this Austin, Texas, charmer falls into. Dallas-based Meredith Ellis, whose résumé includes film sets and stints with legendary designers Bunny Williams and Michael S. Smith, gave the project, a charity show home, its vibrancy and soul. "I'm so much more comfortable in a colourful room," she says, explaining that she imagined herself as the client. "People are afraid of colour, but I wanted to get the point across that colour and pattern can be really livable." Inspired by the fun, layered work of English designer Kit Kemp, Meredith sought to blend southern plantation style with an infusion of British Colonial flair. To keep the show home from feeling staged, she brought each room to life with flea market finds. "I wanted this to feel like an old house with all the weird quirks," she says. "Those are the things that add charm."

"I wanted the mudroom to feel like an old porch that had been screened-in, so I added siding to the wall. Then I painted everything out in an inky blue-grey for drama." —Meredith Ellis

Millwork Colour
Cyberspace
(SW 7076) by
Sherwin-Williams

←

With the multi-patterned and coloured family room adjacent to the kitchen, Meredith took the advice of her mother—also a designer—and gave the eye a place to rest. "The Moroccan tiles are just shimmery enough to give the room depth without screaming at you," she says. A durable quartz countertop mimics the look of soapstone.

Kitchen Cabinet Colour:
Repose Gray (SW 7015) by Sherwin-Williams

YES, YOU CAN!

Upholster the walls: Your favourite fabric can be transformed with a paper backing, adding texture to the room.

↑
Green is a wonderful choice for a dining room. It plays well with warm wood tones, is friendly, and exudes energy even when no one's in the room.

DETAILS WE LOVE

1- High-gloss dark green highlights the fun of a swinging door into the kitchen.

2- Bookshelves in a dining room? Yes, please! Their presence gives the room a multipurpose library vibe.

3- Packed shelves thanks to flea market ceramics and books: "When you colour block books they become like artwork without distracting from the room itself," says Meredith.

4- White slipcovers look fresh against all the intense tones and can be easily removed for a wash between uses.

Shelves + Trim Colour:
Privilege Green (SW 6193) by Sherwin-Williams

"There's a global approach to the sunroom; it's meant to transport you. Shuttered cabinetry, artisanal textiles, rattan furniture, and tropical plants make this a sophisticated place to sit and have a drink with the French doors wide open." —ME

←

EASY, BREEZY, BEAUTIFUL

The earth-toned palette gets infused with deep tones of rust red and cobalt blue inspired by Indian block-print fabrics and Portuguese tile.

→
Every home needs a
well-stocked bar, and
who wouldn't gravitate
to this one with its
pretty blue-and-white
tiles and pottery
collection? Diagonal
slats on cabinet fronts
are a genius move
in keeping with the
room's tropical theme.

→

When committing to a colour, what's the point in going halfway? Meredith bathed the walls, trim, and millwork of the sitting room at the end of the principal bedroom in a soothing shade: "There's something about this blue-celadon colour that's so soothing." A vertical print on the drapes emphasizes the ceiling colour and makes the French doors appear taller than they are.

YES, YOU CAN!

Add a fringe to the bottom edge of roman shades. It's the decorating equivalent of a wink!

"I love to warm up a big, white stone bathroom with drapery and an antique Oushak rug. It still feels clean, but has character and flows with the rest of the house."

—ME

← The intersection of floor and wall tile looks extra crisp and clean—just what you want in a bathroom— without a baseboard.

→ "Matchy matchy" isn't always a forbidden phrase in decorating. Here, in the principal bedroom, a custom nickel bed echoes the trellis-print wallpaper.

SEAFARING STYLE

The boys' room reads like the captain's quarters on a boat, thanks to vintage maps and artwork, and a nautical palette. Glossy beadboard paneling celebrates the angled ceilings instead of trying to make them blend in.

Ceiling Colour
Repose Gray
(SW 7015) by
Sherwin-Williams

Meredith took advantage of the show home's imaginary client by experimenting with a persimmon bedroom. "This would be a stretch for a lot of people, so I wanted to show it in a way that wasn't scary," she says. "It's a spicy orange, but there's enough brown to keep it earthy."

Wall Colour
Cavern Clay (SW 7701) by Sherwin-Williams

YES, YOU CAN!

Use an unexpected colour like brown in a bathroom—just be sure to mix in fresh hits of white and blue to keep it pretty.

Cool idea alert: integrating two prints with applied moulding. "This is how I do tonal," says Meredith. "It's an interesting way to layer a wall, but the greyed tones of the paper-backed fabric keep it simple."

↓
Put an exclamation point on a vignette by matching the trim and millwork to the wallpaper. Here, shades of raspberry, blue, and black in the pillows keep the blush pink paint from feeling too sweet.

↓
Awash in watercolour pinks, the upstairs den is a super-relaxing spot for reading and movie watching. Pieces that reference different eras—a contemporary sectional and table mingle harmoniously with a mid-century modern–style chair and Art Deco wall sconce—give the impression they've been acquired over time.

"MY CLIENTS ARE FEARLESS COLOUR LOVERS, BUT AFTER LIVING IN A SATURATED, JEWEL-TONED HOME FOR DECADES, THEY WANTED A FULL RESET. WE STARTED FRESH, BRIGHTENED UP, AND SHOWCASED THE SOFTER SIDE OF COLOUR."

YES, YOU CAN!

Pull a palette from artwork: Hand-painted botanicals from an antique book dealer became the inspiration for an opal-tinted room accented with tones of blush and salmon.

Next Chapter Chic

DESIGN BY **SARAH RICHARDSON**
PHOTOGRAPHY BY **VALERIE WILCOX**

DESIGN BY **SARAH RICHARDSON**, SARAH RICHARDSON DESIGN

TORONTO, ONTARIO

3,000 SQUARE FEET

3 BEDROOMS

3 BATHROOMS

4 STOREYS

94 YEARS OLD

30 YEARS OF OWNERSHIP

1,200 SQUARE FEET OF NATURAL STONE

472 PANES OF LEADED GLASS

↑
FIRESIDE CHAT

Chaise longues often get relegated to bedrooms where they're rarely used, but not on Sarah's watch. "If the question is, 'Should I put a chaise in my living room?' the answer is, 'Yes, absolutely!'" she says. "One of my favourite things to do is place one beside a fireplace for reading and impromptu dozing."

STATEMENT STORAGE
If you're dealing with a small entry-way, tuck a handy cabinet just inside the living room and it can perform double-duty. A smoky periwinkle cabinet finished in lacquered linen adds a lush note of texture with storage to boot.

THE OWNERS OF this circa 1920s home don't shy away from big challenges and bold statements. For more than 30 years, they loved their jewel-toned home perched atop an urban escarpment with sweeping views of the city. But once their two grown daughters moved out, the house no longer suited their vision of the future. "It was time," says designer Sarah Richardson. "They appreciate contemporary design but were living with '80s contemporary—his office was hunter green! So they decided to purge almost everything and start over." The formula for the top-to-bottom makeover was one part looking back, one part looking forward. "We honoured the architecture but let this place breathe as an open-concept space with more livable colour and texture," says Sarah.

"When a room has as few ingredients as this one does, why not choose something totally unique? We found the hammered brass table base and topped it with leathered Arctic Cloud marble."
—Sarah Richardson

←
The mod-trad mix is a fun formula, but sometimes a room demands restraint. With stunning traditional panel moulding already in place, Sarah chose elegant, streamlined lighting that pays homage to the dining room's architecture rather than going the industrial or boho route.

Cabinet Colour
Wolf Gray
(2127-40) by
Benjamin Moore

"When I asked the owners if they'd consider a strong colour and dynamite backsplash for the kitchen, their answer was, 'Yes, please!' We found the backsplash first, a tile with three types of marble, then drew the gorgeous smoky blue for the cabinets directly from the marble mosaic." —SR

↑
BEST-LAID PLANS

How to make the most of your space when a kitchen island isn't in the cards? Go with a peninsula. In this kitchen's configuration, it offered the most storage and seating, biggest counters, and best overall flow—not to mention some visual drama, jutting out from a full-height pantry. Warm metal pendants pivot so the light can be redirected as needed.

Cabinet Colour
Chantilly Lace
(OC-65) by
Benjamin Moore

↑
The kitchen was the catalyst for the home's renovation. The owners had lived with a dark, cramped space for too long. "The goal for this kitchen was to make it light and bright," says Sarah. "We offset the drama of the blue peninsula with warm white cabinets that wrap the wall behind the range."

YES, YOU CAN!

Turn a nonfunctional bay window into an eating nook with pillows galore. Sarah added a marble top to a vintage Eames table for durability, and placed comfy chairs in front to make the nook an appealing spot for morning coffee or cozy, casual dinners.

"The living room is a testament to how decorating can provide a transition without renovation. We kept the leaded glass windows, changed the floor, and gave everything a fresh coat of paint. Then, we blended warm and cool neutral elements with an eye for softness and texture, always thinking first and foremost, 'How does it feel?'" —SR

↓
To jazz up a neutral room, incorporate subtle, tonal patterns. The chaise by the fireplace (pictured, page 24) is solid, but almost everything else in this room—from the sofa, rug, and chairs, to the windowpanes and vintage travertine table—creates a sense of movement.

↑
BE OUR GUEST

When the guest bedroom comes with its own sitting area, it's not hard to beckon family—in this case, one of the homeowners' two daughters—to "check in" for a while. For the sunwashed space, Sarah chose watery aqua tones and offset them with luxe stone via custom Statuario marble cubes and alabaster lamps.

←

A high-gloss dresser with fluted drawer fronts is a subtle nod to the homeowner's love of Art Deco style, while its curved waterfall surface is soft and pretty.

↓
All-white bathrooms are a classic, but contrast is just as crave-worthy. Sarah pulled the purple-grey vanity colour from the geometric marble shower tile and warmed up the whole scheme with brass fixtures.

Cabinet Colour
Smoke Gray
(2120-40) by
Benjamin Moore

↓
The dreamy principal bedroom is awash in wispy cloud colours and adorned with organic textures and natural motifs, like the origami-like lamp and tree-branch-motif curtain fabric.

DETAILS WE LOVE

1- Any shower detail belongs at eye level; here, Sarah created a band of directional chevron from mosaic tiles sold in 1-foot squares.

2- Integrate a bar with the shower-door fabrication to ensure toweling-off is within easy reach.

3- Streamlined sconces with exaggerated round bulbs look like bubbles or mini-moons—and all the metal tones match!

4- A waterfall vanity brings the eye down to highlight spectacular marble-mosaic floor tiles.

↓
Whitewashing is a great hack to give ready-made furniture a new design vision.
In this case, an Ikea four-poster bed looks custom thanks to a simple brighten-up
treatment. Touches of denim blue in the rug and throw act as secondary neutrals
without interrupting the calming vibe.

YES, YOU CAN!

Drape throws or tapestries over the back
of any headboard for a loose, casual effect.

→
Even in a small space, you can manage to squeeze in a vanity that offers plenty of countertop and storage with an offset sink to accommodate the window and a sconce turned sideways.

"This room is for the youngest daughter, so it feels beachy and natural with a less-is-more approach when it comes to colour." —SR

Cabinet Colour
Stratton Blue
(HC-142) by
Benjamin Moore

↓
Not one, but two islands—a genius idea for frequent entertainers. This layout keeps the crowd away from the cook's zone. Designer Chauncey Boothby had the pendants sprayed one shade lighter than the islands (Wythe Blue (HC-143) by Benjamin Moore). "This way they relate, but don't quite match," she says.

"HOW DO YOU DO COASTAL WITHOUT GETTING CUTESY? MIXING PATTERNS, TEXTURES, AND LAYERS IN A WAY THAT'S NOT MATCHY-MATCHY—PIECES FEEL ACQUIRED OVER TIME."

DESIGN BY CHAUNCEY BOOTHBY
PHOTOGRAPHY BY READ McKENDREE

DESIGN BY
**CHAUNCEY
BOOTHBY**,
CHAUNCEY
BOOTHBY
INTERIORS

COASTAL MAINE

6,400
SQUARE FEET

2 YEARS OLD

8 BEDROOMS

9 BATHROOMS

2 KITCHEN
ISLANDS

2 PARENTS,
4 KIDS

3 LADDERS

→
How do you keep a traditional kitchen from seeming too sweet? Give the breakfast nook some edge. Chauncey paired mid-century-style walnut chairs with a cerused oak table for a chic seating area that glows under the light of an iconic Noguchi paper lantern.

←
Crisp, clean, and classically New England: This three-season home in a small town on the coast of Maine has a wide-open, breezy feel that beckons from the moment you approach its shingled façade.

S ET IN A SMALL village that hugs the Maine coastline, this home looks like it's been kissed by salt air for centuries. In fact, it's a new build designed for a Connecticut family who escapes to this dreamy spot three seasons of the year. For one of the owners, this house represents a homecoming—she grew up in the neighbourhood and longed for a place for her children to connect with extended family nearby. Enter designer Chauncey Boothby, a fellow Maine native who, in collaboration with architect Vincent Falotico, worked to give this family a classic New England experience with a twist. "My client was adamant about making this house unique," says Chauncey. "She didn't want the expected Maine beachhouse with navy blue and nautical motifs." Their winning formula? A combination of soft and bright blues paired with variations on brown—from mushroom to flax and straw—to give the owners coastal style without the clichés. "We made some brave decisions and pushed outside their comfort zones, but that's where the fun comes in," says Chauncey. "While it's easy to play it safe, it's so much more rewarding to play with colour."

→

When the architecture's formal but the family's casual,
add woven rush chairs for a friendly, beachy feel. Modern
lanterns are a fun variation on a theme—Chauncey used more
traditional versions just outside in the entry hall.

↓
Lacquered mushroom-coloured
cabinets make the bar a destination,
especially when set up in a "serve
yourself" style for company.

Lantern Colour
Hague Blue (30)
by Farrow & Ball

YES, YOU CAN!
Highlight
architecture by
painting the trim:
"It's such a fun way
to dress a room
without wall colour
or wallpaper."

**YES,
YOU CAN!**

Incorporate
shiplap
without going
overboard.
Adding it to
the hallway
delivers texture
and durability
when kids are
running in
and out all day.

The great room walls may be white, but the artwork and furnishings infuse the space with bright sea blues, pale aquas, and dusky mauves. A 14- x 19-foot wool rug was Chauncey's starting point—she loves how it adds coziness underfoot. Two ethereal sea-and-sky paintings bring the glorious outdoor views inside.

"My client's favourite colour is soft teal blue, so I gave her a big dose of it with the two sofas. My trick for families is to pick a durable fabric for upholstery, then use a more precious fabric for pillows; it's a win-win."
—Chauncey Boothby

SOFT & SERENE

Cool idea alert: The walk-through shower sits between matching vanities. Chauncey chose polished nickel finishes throughout to make the ensuite look clean, sophisticated, and elegant.

→
Bedding in whisper-soft tones of seafoam and duck egg are warmed up by the ash wood chair frame and a raffia light fixture. Chauncey endorses shiplap but uses it judiciously—like on the ceiling. "It can get overdone, so I stick with strategic accents," she says.

"The principal bedroom has the best views of the ocean so my job was easy—I merely had to enhance it." —CB

BEDROOM ROUNDUP

1- Who wouldn't want to curl up in this window seat? Corals and blush pinks play nicely with light sky blues from the light fixture down to the French-tufted pad on the bench.

2- Wrapping the inside of the bunkroom in shiplap makes it feel cozier for family members who want to curl up after a day at the beach. Purple accents add richness to all the white.

3- "There were so many strong colours in the kids' rooms, I kept the guest room fresh," says Chauncey. A bolster introduces a hint of yellow and green, while everything else is crisp white and indigo.

4- A scalloped headboard, soft roman shades, and a pom-pom quilt are youthful without being childish.

1

2

3

4

1

BATHROOM ROUNDUP

1- While the daughter's ensuite is outfitted in classics, the floor looks like a charming country quilt reinterpreted as tile.

2- A streamlined sailboat painting from the homeowners' existing collection creates a "view" down the sightline. "Art wasn't initially slated for this space, but as soon as I saw it I knew it had to go here," says Chauncey.

3- If you're tempted to flirt with a theme, the powder room's the spot! A nautical sconce and mirror make the tiny space feel shipshape.

"The boys' bunkroom is designed for sleepovers, so we really went for it and pushed the colour with primary brights—if not here, where?" –CB

←

The older boys' bunkroom pulses with youthful, primary colours. In both the bunkroom and bathroom, Chauncey played with red sconces in different shapes and finishes to create a sense of cohesion.

↓

"We were going for a bit of a lifeguard vibe in the two boys' shared bunkroom and ensuite," says Chauncey. Wavy bathroom tiles, *Baywatch* red accents, and even a shark on the wall are subtle nods to the theme. Slim drawers at the base of the bunks maximize storage for bedding or toys.

↓
Bright orangey-red notches up the
energy in the nursery. Pale blue walls
act as a grounding, neutral force to keep
the space bold but not busy.

←
The home's exterior is the definition of "picturesque," thanks to the classic New England roofline, pair of stone chimneys, and white picket fence.

↓
Since the family spends a lot of time here, the husband needed a functional office. "He has an affinity for mid-century modern style but his wife didn't want it to read as too "*Mad Men*," says Chauncey. She paired creamy white walls and traditional millwork (not to mention a library ladder!) with a few iconic mid-century pieces for a happy compromise.

The screened-in porch's stone fireplace was designed to make the new build read as a grand old Maine home. The stone looks like the colours of the dunes while fresh blues reference the water.

"THIS SPACE IS WHERE
YOU CAN BE RELIEVED OF
YOUR FEAR OF COLOUR,
PATTERN, AND LAYERS.
IT'S A FAR MORE LASTING
LOOK THAN YOU'D THINK!"

Colour Theory

EMBRACE HUMOUR

Who says you can't have fun at the office? Not Toronto designer Gillian Gillies, who used the blank canvas of her design firm's office in an industrial building as a place to play with bold colour and pattern. Speaking of bold, you can't miss the fringed leather swing, a souvenir from a trip to São Paolo, Brazil, at the head of the conference table. "If not here, when?" she says with a laugh.

DESIGN BY GILLIAN GILLIES

PHOTOGRAPHY BY VIRGINIA MACDONALD

DESIGN BY
GILLIAN GILLIES,
GILLIAN GILLIES
INTERIORS

TORONTO,
ONTARIO

1,000 SQUARE
FEET

18-FOOT
CEILINGS

3-MONTH
RENOVATION

2-FOOT HIGH
GEORGIAN
FRIEZE

1 SWING

TRY TONAL
Gillian paired the green cabinets with a moody,
historic wallpaper she'd always wanted to use that
had just a kiss of the same green as the paint.
The jute runner was a had-to-have-it find with
modern geometric shapes in black and navy to
help pull out the blue tones.

↓

PICK A STARTING POINT

The green for the kitchen—a 10-foot-high floating structure with a library wall on the other side—
was the first decision Gillian made for the office. It was also the easiest: Green is her favourite
colour. The finished product opened her clients' eyes to the possibilities: "Prior to this, it would
have been a hard sell to convince a client to do intense green millwork. Now, they come in and say,
'Wow, can I have that?'"

Cabinet Colour
Bancha (298)
by Farrow & Ball

APPROACHING **GILLIAN GILLIES** Interiors from the outside, you'd never expect what awaits
behind the door. "This was a concrete and drywall box in an industrial plaza," says the
Scottish-born, Toronto-based designer. "But when you come inside, you're transported to
another place—one that's happy, colourful, and full of my favourite things." In Gillian's happy place,
verdant green millwork mingles with five different wallpapers and tongue-in-cheek flea market
artwork. The colours shouldn't work together and yet, they do. Her goal? To showcase the power of
mixing colours to boost mood or create intimacy. "Too often, I have to drag my clients kicking and
screaming from white to ivory," she says with a laugh. "Here, they can see what it looks like when
you give yourself permission to splash colour and pattern all over the place." Even the FedEx guy
recently proclaimed her office, "like a spa or something," Gillian reports. Mission accomplished!
Here, she shares her lessons for lush, layered, and colourful spaces.

↑
CONSIDER THE VIEW

By moving her desk away from the wall and floating it, Gillian has a more inspiring view of the office's library. Her backdrop is a large-scale abstract floral wallpaper that celebrates the airy ceilings.

1

↑
GET PERSONAL

A black woven hanging is a graphic punctuation mark. "The power of black, especially in a colourful space, can't be underestimated. It has a grounding effect and gives your eye a place to rest."

2

"There's nothing in here that was done just for the sake of doing. Scattered throughout are things from my travels and that's what makes the office feel like home to me."
—Gillian Gillies

DETAILS WE LOVE

1- A custom 2-foot-tall frieze, inspired by the Georgian terrace buildings of Edinburgh, separates the decorated space from the more industrial ceiling.

2- When cabinets aren't in a kitchen, durability's not as important. Inset grasscloth wallpaper for a wow moment of texture and interest.

3- Sliding doors save space when door swings might be a challenge.

4- Brass and walnut accents are a welcome glimmer of warmth against the deep, historic colours used throughout the office.

3

EAT DRINK NAP

4

YES, YOU CAN!
Juxtapose two styles of wallpaper: The walls are a modern floral while the ceiling is a traditional yet quirky gold bumble bee print.

↑

BREAK THE RULES

Black walls in a windowless space? Gillian went for it, spurred on by the Nina Campbell wallpaper she'd been lusting after since it didn't make the cut in a client's project. The bright white of the peonies and zingy green of the marble liven up the dark background and make the barrier-free washroom a highlight instead of an afterthought.

Gallery walls work best within a chosen palette—even if it's not obvious
at first. Gillian gathered some vintage and new pieces, then found a great
pillow fabric that spoke to the recurring tones of ochre, apricot, and pale
aqua. The saffron fringe at the bottom of the daybed is the exclamation point.
"Though there are a lot of contrasting colours in the art, the key recurring
shades are in harmony," Gillian says. "You need a plan. Colour for colour's
sake can be an assault on the senses."

Wall Colour
Studio Green (93) by Farrow & Ball

POOLS
THAT WOW

THE NEW WAY
TO HOLIDAY

CRAVE-WORTHY
CERAMICS

6 SMART IDEAS
FROM SARAH

Global Edit

Our roundup of what's new
and now around the world,
whether you like to live in bold
colour or thrive in neutral.

HAVING A MOMENT

TAKE THE PLUNGE

Thinking about splashing out on the ultimate staycation
spot, or just hoping for a vicarious vacation? Look no further:
We've got inspiration from residential retreats to dreamy
hotel destinations.
—

↓
HAMPTONS HAVEN
By framing a pool with two pergolas, architecture firm KOS+A narrows the
focus on the breathtaking horizon—and creates multiple breezy nooks from
which to enjoy it. PHOTOGRAPHY BY READ McKENDREE

IN FULL VIEW
Sarah Richardson's own pool at Starlight Farm takes a less-is-more approach. The deep grey-blue liner reflects the sky and changes as the light does.
PHOTOGRAPHY BY VALERIE WILCOX

"**S**HOULD WE GET a pool?" More North American families than ever are asking the question as staying home becomes the new going away. Whether you're planning to take that travel fund and invest in a resort-quality pool or just dreaming about it, we're taking you on a trip to some of the most coveted pools in homes and hotels around the world. Grab your virtual passport and get ready to dive in!

VICTORY LAP
Who says pools are just for warm weather? This indoor beauty, designed by Rockside Campbell Design, has all the right ingredients to make jaws drop: a rustic stone wall, black windows and doors, an undulating cedar ceiling, and skylight tubes that frame vignettes of the clouds.
PHOTOGRAPHY BY LORNE BRIDGMAN

MODERN MARVEL
With minimal decking and a linear Workshop APD-designed home as its backdrop, this oh-so-stylish pool looks like the setting of a Slim Aarons photo. The pool creates a perpendicular line with the home's stone columns for an architectural, runway-like effect. PHOTOGRAPHY BY READ McKENDREE

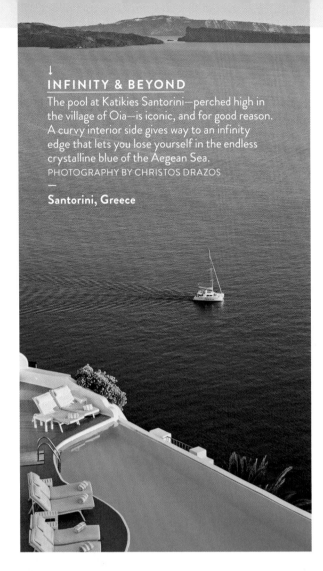

↓
INFINITY & BEYOND
The pool at Katikies Santorini—perched high in the village of Oia—is iconic, and for good reason. A curvy interior side gives way to an infinity edge that lets you lose yourself in the endless crystalline blue of the Aegean Sea.
PHOTOGRAPHY BY CHRISTOS DRAZOS
—
Santorini, Greece

→
PEAK BLISS
At Miramonti Boutique Hotel, it's the ultimate indoor-outdoor pool: Start your swim in the heated saltwater infinity pool under a canopy of rustic wood beams, and emerge to panoramic views of the city of Merano and the Alps beyond at its infinity edge.
—
Hafling, Italy

↓
ROCK ON
Surrounded by canyons, desert, mountains, and mesas, Amangiri Resort's pool is a true natural wonder nestled into the rock of the Grand Staircase-Escalante—protected land that spans nearly one million acres. As the sky changes from apricot to pink, a secluded swim won't be a problem.
PHOTOGRAPHY COURTESY OF AMAN
—
Canyon Point, Utah

→
PATTERN PLAY
Like floating on
a checkerboard,
graphic black and
white tiles at the
super-stylish Brown
Beach House Hotel
invite lazy laps or
a dip at dusk to
watch the sun set
on the glistening
Adriatic Sea.
—
Trogir, Croatia

SUMMER CAMP
FOR GROWN-UPS

Design lovers rejoice! Camping doesn't have to mean roughing it in a rustic (read: rickety) trailer or leaky tent. At AutoCamp, a new concept with locations in California wine country, Yosemite, and Cape Cod, you can check in to one of a fleet of groovy Airstream trailers, or sleep under the stars in a luxury tent. With chic clubhouses and communal areas on site, camping never looked so good and felt so comfy.

—

autocamp.com

PHOTOGRAPHY BY AUBRIE PICK (LEFT), JOHNIE GALL (TOP), CARLI STATSKY (MIDDLE), AUTOCAMP (BOTTOM)

← AIRSTREAM AL FRESCO

Tucked away at the edges of the campground, the trailers have streamlined landscaping that enhance their iconic silver exteriors—and give campers a cool hangout spot.

→ SMALL BUT MIGHTY

The trailers' interiors are bright, minimal, and modern, with upscale bathrooms and kitchenettes. Clever idea alert: A frosted glass door lets light flow through without sacrificing privacy.

← BLANK CANVAS

Be transported away to another world (*Out of Africa* fantasies, anyone?) in a billowy white tent outfitted with a king bed. Black and wood accents give the interior a woodsy industrial vibe.

Oh, Happy Clay!

Turning a piece of clay into a refined, soulful accessory for the home doesn't happen by accident or through a stroke of luck—it's a gift. Here, we celebrate some of the makers producing collectable and covetable pottery that make us say, "Ooh, I want that!"

Cream & sugar, $230

—

One-of-a-kind collection, $225

—

One-of-a-kind collection, $290

—

BERT WALTER & JENNIFER BERNSTEIN

Meilen Ceramics
Tableware | Vases
MEILENCERAMICS.COM

TRAINING GROUND

Bert did a formal potter's apprenticeship in Höhr-Grenzhausen and studied art before opening his Frankfurt atelier in 2000. Jennifer studied printmaking before making the switch to ceramics, with a specific focus on colour research and development. We love seeing how naturally our individual skills come together toward a common goal.

ONE COOL FACT

We met in the Frankfurt airport and have been together ever since.

INTENTION

We want people to notice how a well-made piece makes your daily rituals even more of a pleasure, from how the vessel feels in the hand to how the unexpected colour allows for food to shine more vibrantly.

PRICE RANGE

From $40 to $1,200

ARTIST SPOTLIGHT

Large matte pendant, $795
—
Vases, $300–$750
—

VICTORIA MORRIS

Victoria Morris Pottery
Bowls | Vases | Lamps
VICTORIAMORRISPOTTERY.COM

TRAINING GROUND
I have about 30 years of throwing experience at this point. I really wish I'd majored in ceramics in college, but sometimes we take the slower path forward. One thing I find so incredible about ceramics is that no matter your level of experience or education, there's always more to learn if you're curious.

INSPIRATION
I'm most often looking to Japanese pottery and mid-century makers of all kinds.

CREATIVE PROCESS
When I sit down to throw, I plan on throwing a family of work that relates to one another with a focus on line and proportion. But I think I love trimming the most—it's the part of the process where you really get to refine your piece and make it sing.

PRICE RANGE
$120 to $3,000

Clockwork Orange, $2,900
—
Folded ceramic objects, $1,500–$3,000
—
Earthenware Ferrari series, from $2,000
—

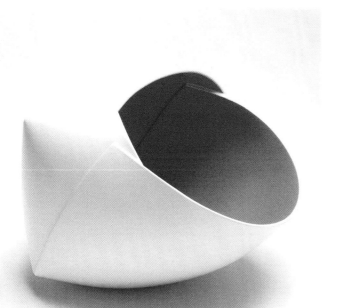

ANN VAN HOEY

Ann Van Hoey Ceramics
Bowls | Trays
ANNVANHOEY-CERAMICS.BE

TRAINING GROUND

At university in Belgium, I studied Economics. At age 45, I decided to take lessons in ceramics at the Institute for Arts and Craft in Mechelen, my hometown, and earned my diploma at 50.

CREATIVE PROCESS

I'm inspired by mathematics with its infinite possibilities. I start by making a perfect geometrical shape with thin slabs of clay—either a hemisphere or an oval form—then I cut pieces with my big scissors to fold and create a new, attractive object.

ONE COOL FACT

The objects from my "Earthenware Ferrari" series are not glazed, but professionally sprayed with Ferrari red automotive paint in a body shop.

WHERE TO BUY

New York: jlohmanngallery.com;
Massachussetts: lucylacoste.com;
London, UK: maudandmabel.com.

PRICE RANGE

$1,500 to $7,000

Vase, $30
—
Bowls, $18–$52
—

LALESE STAMPS

Lolly Lolly Ceramics
Mugs | Bowls
LOLLYLOLLYCERAMICS.COM

A selection of pieces from Lalese Stamps's 100 Day Project, in which she challenged herself to create a completely different mug for 100 days straight.

TRAINING GROUND
I studied advertising and graphic design, and I look for inspiration in furniture and architecture. I think my design skills shine through in my ceramic pieces because I always keep my eyes open for inspiration in my surroundings.

CREATIVE PROCESS
My favourite step is throwing on the wheel, but of course sketching and planning a piece is pretty fun, too. When someone buys one of my pieces I want them to feel pride.

ONE COOL FACT
Lolly is a nickname given to me by one of my high school teachers. I surely had no idea at the time that it would be the identity of my business one day.

PRICE RANGE
$35 to $80

100 Day Project one-of-a-kind mugs, prices available upon request

CHRISTIAN ROY

Christian Roy Atelier
Mugs | Bowls | Vases
CHRISTIANROY-ATELIER.COM

TRAINING GROUND
I studied ceramics in Quebec City and graduated in 1998. Then, because I wasn't yet ready to make my own collection, I worked for different potters for about 15 years. After that formative experience, I was ready to launch my own work.

INTENTION
When I create a new item, I adjust and make it better until I can say, "It's in the collection!" My goal is to create skilled, handmade pottery that makes food look better. When someone buys one of my pieces, I want them to touch and use it, and to realize all the details are there for a reason.

ONE COOL FACT
From age 8 to 21, I was a figure skater. I've been spinning for a long time!

PRICE RANGE
$16 to $70

JILL ROSENWALD

Jill Rosenwald Studio
Bowls | Vases | Trays | Lamps
JILLROSENWALD.COM

TRAINING GROUND

I studied Liberal Arts at Hamilton College, but experience has been my best teacher. In running a small business, one needs to wear lots of hats and see what works.

INSPIRATION

Inspiration is all around me and often found in the most unlikely places. The lens through which I see the world highlights any and all things that interest me, be it the curlicue on a piece of lace or the red and blue stripes on the side of a US Mail truck.

INTENTION

When people buy my pieces, they're buying something bigger than that—they're now part of my story and my studio. My sincere wish is that this new shiny piece will bring them pleasure and joy for many years to come.

PRICE RANGE

$60 to $800

Le Bird Cache pot,
$220

—

Café au lait bowls and
small bowls, $70–$88

—

PALETTE CLEANSERS

Will your room be calm and quiet, or fun and fresh? Sarah Richardson shares 6 foolproof formulas for decorating with confidence.

PHOTOGRAPHY BY VALERIE WILCOX

—

All furniture and rugs available at
sarahrichardson.palliser.com

NEUTRAL

1- **Wow-factor wallcovering + pared-down furnishings = instant impact.** Liven up your work-from-home situation with modernist scribble in the simplest palette of cream and black.

2- **When in doubt, start from the ground up.** A tonal flatweave rug sets the scene for a neutral dining room that's anything but ho-hum.

3- **If your idea of neutral isn't high contrast, let barely there tones of blush and sand invite relaxation.** It's a winning scheme for a modern beachhouse-inspired bedroom.

4

COLOUR

4- **Looking for a new-and-now mix?** Marry a colour that's in your comfort zone with one new trend accent. In this case, teal has long-lasting appeal while warm honey tones make the palette current.

5- **If there's a colour you love, use it in varying intensities.** For this true-blue denim palette, the floor is stonewashed, the sofa is raw and inky, and the walls are airy chambray.

6- **Ombré all day! Play with thin, builder-basic strips of wood and space them out irregularly, then highlight the variation with paint.** The rule is, there is no rule. Though fun, it's not forever: Change the pillows and repaint the wall and you have a neutral space.

5

6

"SOME PROPERTIES ARE CHALLENGING, BUT THIS ONE FELT LIKE AN OPTIMISTIC, HAPPY HOUSE FROM THE FIRST MINUTE I WALKED IN. SURROUNDED BY NATURE AND FILLED WITH AMAZING LIGHT, THE LATE-'80s RANCH JUST NEEDED A NEW LEASE ON LIFE."

Ranch Revival

The home's siting means it gets light from both east and west while being surrounded by a football field–sized yard and charming split-rail fence.

DESIGN BY SARAH RICHARDSON

PHOTOGRAPHY BY VALERIE WILCOX

DESIGN
BY **SARAH
RICHARDSON**,
SARAH
RICHARDSON
DESIGN

SINGHAMPTON,
ONTARIO

2,650 SQUARE
FEET

3 BEDROOMS

3 BATHROOMS

13 SLABS OF
MARBLE AND
QUARTZ

1.8 ACRES

4 CLERESTORY
WINDOWS

24-INCH
SUNKEN LIVING
ROOM

"LIKE A COOL LOFT** in the country"—that's how designer Sarah Richardson describes her first impression of the single-storey ranch, a builder-kit home that had good bones and great vibes but needed a serious front-to-back update. "I was so drawn to the light flooding in, the one-level open floor plan, and the privacy afforded by a woodlot out back," she says of the investment property she and her husband, Alexander Younger, tackled for their *Design Life* YouTube series. Sarah's goal was to renovate as effectively and affordably as possible, while maintaining the home's character and quality of construction. Keeping the palette limited to white, black, and grey in the living spaces seemed like the best approach: "I felt from the beginning that no colour was the way to go," she explains. "When everything is hushed and simple, it makes the rooms feel bigger and allows the retro architecture to take centre stage."

→
The sunken living room feels cool and loungey, and Sarah kept much of its original features intact, including a small pass-through that connects to a foyer closet where firewood is stored. New floors, a marble mantel and hearth, and chimney breast were the biggest changes. Decorative additions—like a nubbly rug designed by Sarah, wool chair, cowhide ottoman, and slipcovered sofa—nudge the room into "never want to leave" territory.

"I'm not normally a fan of diagonals, but the existing tongue-and-groove panelling emphasized the ceiling line and had a modern country feel. I knew that once they were painted white, it would be a great envelope for pared-back design." —Sarah Richardson

DETAILS WE LOVE

1- A cabinet at the left side of the island faces the dining room and patio doors, turning otherwise dead space into added storage.

2- The party-sized kitchen features a 10-foot-long peninsula to give the kitchen multiple prep surfaces and define the kitchen and dining room.

3- Dark cabinets work best in a velvety, matte finish—gloss would be too glam for the country setting.

4- Pick a stone waterfall counter for a high-traffic throughway; it's more durable and won't chip or scratch the way painted cabinets would.

YES, YOU CAN!
Turn a pendant into a sconce—a gold-tinted reflector bulb and wire cage cast a unique pattern at night.

→
Three sets of
30-inch-wide
drawers look more
streamlined and
sophisticated than a
mix of drawers and
cabinets, especially
when it's a main
sightline upon
entering the house.

4

↑
Big-box store cabinetry isn't just for kitchens!
In an open-concept space, matching cabinets
create a custom 10-foot-wide credenza for
cohesiveness, and are topped by the same
white Caesarstone as the kitchen counters.
Outdoor dining chairs are a great solution for
families: they're stackable, comfortable, and
easy to move outside in a pinch.

YES, YOU CAN!

Use ready-made linen drapery panels and have them sewn into romans for an inexpensive alternative to fabric by the yard.

↓

If you've practiced restraint in the main spaces, have fun in the private ones! "The bedrooms in this house weren't blessed with high ceilings or amazing architecture, so that's when I like to leverage wallpaper," says Sarah. Placing the bed in front of windows made the most sense, layout-wise, but the sightline stays airy thanks to glass tabletops that align with the windowsill height.

Wallpaper
Caro Eggshell Polka Dots by Brewster Home Fashions

↑
LET'S MAKE A DEAL

A marble-surplus shop is your friend for finding deals—Sarah scored this pistachio marble for $5/sq. ft. and used it to create a chunky, 2-½-inch counter.

↓
Turn leftover materials into clever design solutions with outside-the-box thinking. A guest bedroom headboard was fashioned from bed slats, while the bedside table was made from extra cabinetry and topped with scrap lumber. The pattern for the rug, part of Sarah's own product collection, is called "Robin's Palette" and is based on a watercolour her eldest daughter painted at age 8.

Wallpaper:
Tia Blue Texture
by Brewster
Home Fashions

THE LOW DOWN

(*Above left*) A sloped ceiling meant clearance for a tub was tight. The solution? Sink it down, then create a crisp edge of mitred white quartz and marble.

SLAB HAPPY

(*Below left*) Marble slabs seem ultra-luxe but can be less expensive to install than tiles, which require more labour. Save by finding unusual surplus pieces or splurge on your dream marble!

DOOR PRIZE

(*Above right*) A slim, floating armoire creates an intersection of heights and depths, while providing ample extra storage for bathroom essentials, towels, and supplies.

SIDE HUSTLE

(*Below right*) Bathrooms don't have to be symmetrical: "Everything about this house is about the roofline and sloped ceilings, so we did a sloped backsplash and moved the mirror and sink to one side," says Sarah.

YES, YOU CAN!

When space is tight, use a pair of closet doors to reduce the swing clearance needed.

Wallpaper
Hoppet Grey Folk
by Brewster
Home Fashions

↓
In the basement bathroom, a tall mirror makes the ceiling seem higher. Sarah used less than $200 of marble to make a 5-foot-wide block vanity.

"For a riff on tongue and groove, we installed industrial slot wall, which you'd normally see running horizontally in a store display, and sprayed it blue to create a cozy bed nook." —SR

←
The quest for found space never stops: Sarah decommissioned a cramped closet in the principal bedroom, and gave half the square footage to the bunkroom and the other half to the principal bath.

"The basement was divided into two spaces, so we opened it up and installed a glass stair enclosure and railings to let light flow through and cut down on sound floating upstairs from the media room." —SR

YES, YOU CAN! Make your own stylish ping-pong table with online-order legs and painted cabinet-grade plywood top—the vintage net was sprayed pale grey.

←

To save money, consider framing out the ceiling with flat stock trim pieces. "It adds interest, and we spaced them out such that we didn't need to hire a drywall taper," says Sarah.

→

Floating vinyl flooring with foam backing is a foolproof basement-floor choice—inexpensive, sound-deafening, and easy to clean.

↓

Flank a fireplace with two comfy chairs for conversing and cocktail-sipping. The existing gas fireplace was reclad in remnant marble for a new, modern look.

"MY CLIENTS FELL HEAD OVER HEELS IN LOVE WITH THIS WATERFRONT NEW BUILD AND BROUGHT US ON TO MAKE IT FEEL LIKE IT HAD ALWAYS BEEN THERE—AN INHERITED HOME STEEPED IN TRADITION AND DECORATED WITH AN EYE FOR CASUAL AND STYLISH LIVING."

Classic on the Cape

DESIGN BY LISA THARP

PHOTOGRAPHY BY READ McKENDREE

↑
The manicured grounds of the quintessential Cape Cod summer home overlook a saltwater pond. A dip in the infinity pool is the perfect end of a day spent boating on the Bay.

DESIGN BY
LISA THARP,
LISA THARP
DESIGN

CHATHAM,
MASSACHUSETTS

5,850 SQUARE
FEET

7 BEDROOMS

6 BATHROOMS

2 PARENTS,
2 KIDS

1-YEAR
RENOVATION

1 OUTDOOR
SHOWER

1 INFINITY
POOL

WHEN BOSTON-BASED designer Lisa Tharp meets new clients, she does a deep dive. "We uncover their preferences, but we also ask a ton of questions that seemingly have nothing to do with design," says Lisa. Through that very process, she learned two key pieces of information that would drive the design of this shingled house by the sea. First, that the husband's favourite colour was blue. Second, that the wife named a legendary First Lady as her style icon. "We started calling the house, 'Jackie O on the Water,' and it became the perfect metaphor for all our decisions," says Lisa. "We were looking to create a casual yet effortlessly chic home that Jackie herself would've been happy to visit." The out-of-state owners, a young family with two children, envisioned this as the spot where they'd spend precious summer months, filling the home with the sounds of entertaining and play dates. Lisa maximized seating (and sleeping quarters) and brought in a colour scheme inspired by the blues of the hydrangea bushes and the Bay outside to give these busy owners the tranquil retreat they craved.

← Silvered cedar shake shingles and a wide front porch with substantial columns make the owners' summertime arrival as welcoming as possible.

↓ Designer Lisa Tharp chose restful colours to reflect the surroundings—namely the expansive water views. "Our palette ranges from a variety of light to medium blues and greys, with some warm hits in there to keep the rooms feeling inviting and balanced," she says.

↓
ROOM WITH A VIEW

When the windows double as the entertainment, stick with solid upholstery, drapes, and rugs, and let the pattern come from texture, artwork, flowers, and books. A pair of hydrangea-blue doors acts as the heart of the colour scheme, but they also have an architectural purpose. "It's a long, narrow space including living, dining, and kitchen, and the ceilings can seem lower," says Lisa. "By adding those doors in the middle of that long run, we visually elevated the ceilings by using one of the strongest colours in the palette."

"We updated the fireplace surround with Colonial paneling and painted it a pale, warm grey to call it out as an architectural feature. Candle sconces, a new production of an historic style, help the cause, too."

—Lisa Tharp

↑
An armless baby blue sofa—neither usual nor
expected—looks effortlessly chic and natural,
like a sleeveless shirt in summertime.

←
Forgoing a sofa and surrounding a round
ottoman with chairs and a daybed maximizes
seating—and comfort—for entertaining.
Tharp used a different fabric for every piece
of furniture, except for the swivel chairs,
which she covered in a touchable bouclé.
Adding beams to the tray ceiling draws the
eye up and gives the room a sense of history.

CLASSIC ON THE CAPE

**YES,
YOU CAN!**
Mount small
artwork to the
front of a bookcase
for an intimate,
eye-catching
moment.

"In all the kitchens I design, I hide every appliance except for the range. That way, it becomes the hearth of the kitchen." —LT

↑
A surfboard-shaped dining table is a casual, beachy addition to the open dining room. A double-arm pendant matches its elongated shape.

←
Detailed millwork continues into the kitchen. Installing astragal moulding extends the crown molding above the cabinets onto the ceiling. "It's just one small touch that allows your eye to travel north," says Lisa. A slab of Pietra Cardosa marble behind the range creates a strong vertical element to mirror the fireplace on the opposite side of the long, narrow room.

DETAILS WE LOVE

1- When foggy grey and soft white stripes meet in the centre of the angled ceiling, it creates a mesmerizing pattern.

2- An oversized lantern gives the room a visual punchline. "Because the ceiling is so dramatic, all the angles now direct the eye to this focal point," says Lisa.

3- Simple, white roll-up sail shades play to the sailboat-meets-tent theme in an unfussy way.

4- Instead of placing a daybed at the foot of the main bed, look to the window. Here, an antique Swedish daybed offers a dreamy spot for boat watching on Crows Pond.

Wall Fabric
Oasis Linen Stripe in
Fog by Schumacher

"I'm not a big camper,
but as soon as I stood in
the principal bedroom
and saw water on three
sides, I channeled a
Thoreau-style tent on a
pond—a full-on getaway
from everyday troubles."
—LT

↓
Skirting the bedside table in matching fabric allows it to recede visually and offers peekaboo storage tucked underneath.

↓
Be mindful of sightlines—what do you want to see when you enter your bedroom? Lisa created a focal point with an upholstered folding screen, then hung a painting salon-style with a satin ribbon for an added layer.

→

HIDDEN CHARMS

Though this shell-pink alcove was designed for a child, it's cozy enough to have adult appeal. Underneath the loft bed is a play space; the bed is accessed via a step behind the drapery. "I would happily stay here," says Lisa. "It's sophisticated enough to grow with a young child, or to suit an overnight guest."

"In the extra bedrooms we had more free reign to create little jewel box stories. The common areas are calm, so as we moved further away we could have more fun since they're not used every day." —LT

←
Four can sleep toe-to-toe in the bunkroom surrounded by playful wide-striped wallpaper. Lisa railroaded ticking stripe fabric on the mattress upholstery to match the horizontal orientation of the wallpaper.

SLEEPING BEAUTIES

Hand-blocked fabric and wallpaper by a local artist depicts a mermaid's purse—the shark embryo sac often found on area beaches—and was the jumping-off point for the room's inky-charcoal and tan colour scheme.

Wall Fabric
Mermaid's Purse by
Design No. Five

↓
The oceanside first-floor guest suite was appointed as though it were a second principal bedroom.
"We did an all-neutral treatment, so it was just about layering in texture and adding a little romance
with a breezy canopy," says Lisa.

↑
Black windows give an unexpected graphic punch to a historic home. Paired with solid drapes that match the walls, the effect is crisp and enveloping. "I used to be a big 'print on the windows' person, but now I'm finding that solid drapes are tidy and easy to decorate around," says designer Katie Rosenfeld. A mix of textures both soft and nubbly, and shapes traditional and modern, give the room its eclectic appeal.

"DOING A 'NO COLOUR' HOUSE IS MUCH HARDER THAN IT LOOKS. THE KEY PIECES ARE ALL WHITE, CREAM, GREY, CAMEL, AND BLACK—WITH STRATEGIC HITS OF PATTERN THROUGH WALLPAPER AND ART. THE END RESULT IS A COZY PLACE FOR THIS FAMILY TO COCOON."

Tudor Twist

DESIGN BY **KATIE ROSENFELD**

PHOTOGRAPHY BY **READ McKENDREE**

DESIGN BY	BOSTON,	2.5 BATHROOMS	1 FIREPLACE
KATIE	MASSACHUSETTS		REMOVED
ROSENFELD,		2 PARENTS,	
KATIE	2,500 SQUARE	3 KIDS	3 WALLPAPER
ROSENFELD	FEET		PATTERNS
& COMPANY		1-YEAR	
	3 BEDROOMS	RENOVATION	

↓
Talk about working with what you've got: The house had a rounded door but no front porch. A custom (and ultra-charming) new Dutch door allows the owners to open just the top; this way, breezes flow through and make the house feel more open to the neighbourhood.

Door + Stair Colour
Off-Black (57) by Farrow & Ball

DESIGNER KATIE ROSENFELD was in the car on the way to an appointment when she got the call from her longtime clients: "Please come see this house and tell us if you think we should buy it!" She turned the car around and zipped over to a desirable street in Boston's Jamaica Plains neighbourhood, the very street her clients, a couple with two college-age children and one in middle school, had always wanted to call home. "By the end of the visit, I was convinced they should buy it, but the wife was convinced they shouldn't," says Katie with a laugh. "It was a very dark and dingy Tudor Revival, but I felt we could turn this ugly duckling into a swan." Once the renovation was complete, Katie turned her attention to brightening up the interior. She painted everything, from the baseboard up to the ceiling, the same warm white: Pointing (2003) by Farrow & Ball. The city home's neutral scheme of white, cream, beige, grey, black, and camel was by design, to contrast with their colourful Cape Cod getaway. "We used a lot of restraint to arrive at a home that was contemporary yet warm, with a little bit of strategic colour and pattern through art, wallpaper, and pillows," says Katie.

When trying to achieve a contemporary balance in a traditional home, use the simplest and thinnest frames on artwork for a lighter, more streamlined look.

Rather than put an addition on the back of the house, the owners decided to focus their budget on making the house, and particularly the kitchen, the best it could be. Inspired by British design, the kitchen is spare and serene—not showy—with accents of black and the warm gleam of brass for personality.

DETAILS WE LOVE

1- A single brass sconce draws the eye up to the ceiling, and provides valuable task—and mood—lighting.

2- On the peninsula, an exposed towel bar and brass foot rail inject a bit of British pub style.

3- Want a surface stone that looks like marble but behaves like granite? Quartz designed to look like marble delivers the best of both worlds: gorgeous veining with durability.

4- Encasing the range hood in drywall and wrapping it with crown molding suited the kitchen's less-is-more approach: "Making it quiet is prettier than making it stand out," says Katie.

5- When storing glassware and serving pieces, consider adding a decorative touch. Antique brass mesh dresses up cabinet fronts, adding texture and warmth.

↓

Two graphic works of art by Jane Timberlake Cooper bring both quietude and height to the space between two windows. An abstract sculpture is placed in front for a monochromatic layer that's spare, yet rich and textured.

→

A streamlined Parsons-style table and inky blue-black console give the room some gutsy contrast against the classic herringbone floors. "I chose a sculptural instead of statement-y pendant that's basically a glass tube," Katie says of the Roll & Hill fixture. "Because it runs the length of the table, it's unobtrusive and doesn't block the view."

"I always mix woods, just like I mix metals. When everything matches it looks too much like a furniture showroom. Instead, you want a space to have depth and variation."
—KATIE ROSENFELD

↓

Looking to add a stylish bar cart to your space? Editing is key! A well-curated collection of bottles, glasses, and accessories make this brass-and-glass cart both functional and beautiful.

Wallpaper
Les Baobabs
Amoureux in Alina
by Zak + Fox

↓
A modern floral print on a gunmetal-grey
background gives the powder room a
traditional note, along with the unlacquered
brass faucet, where the vanity, mirror,
and sconce are quite streamlined—part
of Katie's past-meets-present vision.

YES, YOU CAN!

Move the piano upstairs: By placing it
in the stairwell's second-storey nook, the
sound of music flows throughout the house.

→
Floating a low-slung bed in front of windows
and formal drapes gives the room a cozy
vibe. "We opted for vertical drapes because
roman shades would have looked like one
big horizontal plane," explains Katie.

"We wanted the principal bedroom to have a note of warmth and old-world luxury, so a classic Fortuny ceiling fixture was the perfect thing."

—KR

↓
To make mixed metals work, Katie used brass on both the vanity hardware and light fixtures, while all the plumbing is classic chrome.

↓
In the guest room, a rich accent of cognac leather takes the edge off grey, black, and white.

Wallpaper
Peony (BP 2303)
by Farrow & Ball

↓
This is the only room
in the house where
Katie used a different
colour for the trim
and millwork—
Ammonite (274)
by Farrow & Ball,
an understated grey.

YES, YOU CAN!

Run a shelf right across the wall.
The couple's middle-school-aged
daughter can be the curator
of an ever-changing display;
the shelf makes it look chic
instead of cluttered.

Wallpaper
Blommen Print
in Black by
Schumacher

↑
Black and white can
be fun and friendly.
The wallpaper's
hand-drawn,
illustrated look
celebrates artistry
with a touch of
softness and whimsy.

→
Who says you have
to stick with ready-
made tile patterns?
Penny tiles, sold
in sheets, are easy
to swap out for
contrasting colours,
allowing you to
create your own
DIY look.

"THIS HOUSE IS NESTLED IN UNDULATING HILLS THAT ROLL TO THE SOUTH, SO THE MANDATE IN EACH AND EVERY ROOM WAS TO KEEP IT SPARE, FREE OF COLOUR AND CLUTTER, AND LET THE VIEWS AND NATURAL LIGHT BE THE WOW FACTOR."

Alpine Farmhouse

←
Nickel-gap boards—a crisp, modern alternative to shiplap—create a textural backdrop in a minimal living room. A variety of small-scale prints on pillows act like artwork when the walls are an intentional blank canvas.

DESIGN BY **SARAH RICHARDSON**
PHOTOGRAPHY BY **VALERIE WILCOX**

DESIGN
BY **SARAH
RICHARDSON**,
SARAH
RICHARDSON
DESIGN

CREEMORE,
ONTARIO

4,500 SQUARE
FEET

2 PARENTS, 2
KIDS, 2 POODLES

6 BEDROOMS

4.5 BATHROOMS

360-DEGREE
VIEWS

5 YEARS OF
RENTING

5 YEARS OF
DREAMING +
PLANNING

15 MONTHS
OF BUILDING

S **OMETIMES, A PROPERTY** works its way into your soul. The owners of this late-1800s redbrick farmhouse had spent 10 wonderful years here—as seasonal renters. After years of looking for a similar spot in the area, they had a light bulb moment. "The location has all the charm you'd want from the country: a driveway flanked by a canopy of trees, a white picket fence, the sounds of crickets and bullfrogs—and the place of their dreams was here, not anywhere else," says designer Sarah Richardson. "Rather than move on, they were able to purchase the property, stay put, and add on." Sarah's mandate? To help unify the 148-year-old original house with a modern addition and give the couple and their two daughters a laid-back, loungey getaway with a twist. "The husband is of Swiss descent, so we brought in some European charm with a warm Scandi palette of oatmeal, wheat, flax, camel, and mushroom, and some Alpine-inspired accents." Now, the house is an enveloping home base to welcome these outdoor enthusiasts when the day is done.

← If you love something, bring it home. The authentic reproduction Tyrolean chairs with heart motif were on the client's wish list—a nod to happy times spent as a family in Switzerland.

↓ Tuck a stylish chair in a sunlit spot for the ultimate morning coffee break. A curvy-armed, caned chair fits the bill and nicely accents the white oak waterfall counter, while a vintage painting brings the outdoors in.

← A modern woodstove anchors the large kitchen space and radiates heat throughout the open-concept main floor. Since the kitchen is located in the nearly 150-year-old section of the house, the structure dictated placement of the stove; it now sits in front of the door to the original house porch and in front of a hidden pantry room.

"There's no TV required in this living room because when you're sitting on the sofa, you're going between two channels: the fireplace and these amazing views."

—Sarah Richardson

↑
Nature is always neutral. Moody sky blues liven up the niche above a floating audio cabinet; the artwork is by a local artist who captures the ever-changing landscape.

←
"We considered hundreds of different stones for the fireplace, but this one had warm, neutral tones that reminded us of the land and sky around the property," says Sarah. "It's polished but has an incredible softness." When space permits, consider extending the hearth to include a bench and firewood niche beneath.

"This kitchen is a bridge between the old part of the house and the new addition. Our clients' brief was to make it as quiet as possible, so we kept everything white and layered in some white oak and Arabescato marble, with tones of gold and mushroom, for warmth." —SR

DETAILS WE LOVE

1- Even simple kitchens can be artful: Here, a collection of salt-glazed pottery looks like a still-life painting on white oak accent shelves.

2- Contemporary pendants by Zac Ridgely appear to float over the island and cast an ethereal glow.

3- Wonder how to make a vent hood disappear? Clad it in millwork that's lacquered to match the cabinets.

4- Stools are covered in buttery camel-coloured leather to make them blend in with the white oak island rather than jump out.

YES, YOU CAN!

Paint an entire house the same colour, from the trim to the walls and ceiling. "My go-to is White on White by ICI/Glidden/Dulux," says Sarah. "It never looks too yellow or blue."

Serenity now? You bet. Simple and free of adornment, the dining room is a soothing and sophisticated space both to gather and spend solo time. Exposed floor joists from the second storey make an architectural statement as two George Nelson bubble saucer pendants up the Zen factor. As for the custom table, it's a streamlined take on a classic trestle table, and made from 160-year-old barn floorboards.

"Think about creating destinations in every room to lure you in at different times of day. The husband is an early riser, so we placed two comfy swivel chairs in front of the dining room's wraparound windows; it's a perfect spot to watch the sunrise." –SR

"If you're decorating with a tonal palette, think texture, texture, texture. In the charcoal, cement, and cream principal bedroom, you'll find wool, felt, and embroidery—everything is cozy and touchable." –SR

↓
SHADES OF GREY

To keep the principal bedroom ultra-clean, Sarah chose a bed with integrated side tables to eliminate extra furniture legs and keep the sightlines clutter-free. Encaustic works of art by Sue McNenly draw the eye up to the peak of the airy room's roofline.

YES, YOU CAN!

Make use of a narrow space by floating a bench. Nestled between the walls, the support is clad in a leftover piece of oak flooring and upholstered in a fabric remnant.

↑
Bathroom design guidance: Art is always a good idea! A photograph by
Dean West creates a focal point and feels like another window into a natural
world. Black slate floors add contrast and ground the bathroom.

←
The staircase was
designed to be a
standout feature
and celebrate
the honesty of
construction.
Solid oak treads
create a zigzag
profile, while
hidden touch-
latch dining
room pantry
cupboards tuck
neatly under the
floating glass
stair enclosure.

YES, YOU CAN!

Install a frameless sheet of mirror for a clean, modern look. The finishing detail? Mount the sconces on top.

**YES,
YOU CAN!**

Choose sky-
view inspired
pale blue stone
for a small
bathroom
counter—it's
the ideal place
to take a risk.

"The girls' rooms feature
a little more colour, but
the tones are muted and
earthy; there's nothing
you wouldn't see right
outside the window." –SR

←
SWEET DREAMS

A layered bed with just a hint of
pattern, thanks to textiles and art,
makes one of the daughter's rooms
feel young, fresh, and natural.

←

COZY CHALET

Playing on the home's alpine motif, Sarah added a modern white oak table, wooly sheep sculpture, and tundra-inspired photography with rustic salmons and greys she picked up in the pillow.

↓
How to create a mudroom for the family who plays hard?
Install a durable, vein-cut limestone floor, and build a
solid, white oak bench with spacers for wet clothing and
equipment. "These guys are active skiiers, bikers, and
horseback riders, so it's all gear, all the time," says Sarah.

↓
Nickel-gap walls frame out the basement's infrared sauna—a must-visit destination after chilly afternoons of walking, skiing, or skating.

Collected Source Guide

DESIGNER DIRECTORY
(In order of appearance)

Meredith Ellis Design
meredithellisdesign.com

Sarah Richardson Design
sarahrichardson
design.com

Chauncey Boothby
Interiors
chaunceyboothby.com

Gillian Gillies Interiors
gilliangillies.com

KOS+A
kosullivan.com

Rockside Campbell
Design
rockside.ca

Workshop/APD
workshopapd.com

Lisa Tharp Design
lisatharp.com

Katie Rosenfeld &
Company
katierosenfeld
design.com

"SOUTHERN CHARM," pages 4 to 21
GENERAL: Architect: Chris Sanders, sandersarchitecture.com | Builders: Catherine & David Wilkes, davidwilkesbuilders.com | James Showroom: all textiles and paper-backed fabric (except dining room chair slipcovers and sitting room sofa), jamesshowroom.com.

LIVING ROOM: Arteriors: Celerie Kemble floor lamp, arteriors.com.

MUDROOM: Sherwin-Williams: Cyberspace SW 7076 millwork paint, sherwin-williams.com.

KITCHEN: Sherwin-Williams: Repose Gray SW 7015 cabinet colour, sherwin-williams.com.

DINING ROOM: Sherwin-Williams: Privilege Green SW 6193 shelves and trim colour, sherwin-williams.com.

ORANGE BEDROOM: Sherwin-Willi ͜ ͜ ͜ ͜: Cavern Clay SW 7701 wall colour, sherwin-williams.com.

"NEXT CHAPTER CHIC," pages 22 to 39
GENERAL: First Class Flooring: Quarter Sawn White Oak, firstclassflooring.ca | Glidden: White On White 30GY 88/014 trim paint, glidden.com.

DEN: Tonic Living: roman shades (Mila Dot Fabric), tonicliving.ca | Noir Furniture: Baas Sconce, noirfurniturela.com | Client's own: artwork and frames | EQ3: Oma 2-Piece Sectional Sofa, eq3.com | Bungalow 5: Elba Lounge Chair, bungalow5.com | West Elm: Origami Coffee Table, westelm.ca | Around the Block: pink glass bowl and orange cube, aroundtheblock.com | Tonic Living: pillow fabric (Valentia Velvet Rosewood, Lily Fabric Peony and Passagio Blush), tonicliving.ca | Elte Mkt: Beaker Blush Rug, eltemkt.com | CB2: white vases, cb2.ca | Dulux: Opal 30YY 79/053 wall paint, dulux.com.

DINING ROOM: Eli Barr: artwork, instagram.com/ebarr56 | Circa Lighting: Hackney Large Chandelier and Hackney Buffet Lamp, circalighting.com | Elte Mkt: Nouvel Beige/Grey Rug, eltemkt.com | Bungalow 5: Stockholm Oval Dining Table Base and Cameron 4 Door Cabinet, bungalow5.com | DiNuovo Granite & Marble: marble fabrication, dinuovo.ca | Sarah Richardson Design custom furniture: Nik Dining Chairs, sarahrichardsondesign.com | Premier Prints: fabric on dining chairs (Scott Living Grace Quartz Grey), premierprintsinc.com | Around

the Block: vase, aroundtheblock.com | CB2: bowl, cb2.ca | Benjamin Moore: Horizon OC-53 wall paint, benjaminmoore.com.

KITCHEN: Lavish Kitchens + Fine Cabinetry: cabinetry and island fabrication, lavishkitchens.ca | Upper Canada Specialty Hardware: Cabinet Edge 6" Pull & Trail Pull, ucshshowroom.com | TAPS Bath: Blanco Radius Undermount Sink, Franke FF3450 Stainless Steel Faucet, Blanco Rondo Sink in bar, Franke FFB3450 Stainless Steel Faucet in bar, tapsbath.com | Saltillo: Tracks Calacatta Moonstone backsplash tile and 12" x 24" Sky Blue Honed floor tile, saltillo-tiles.com | DiNuovo Granite & Marble: table top marble fabrication, dinuovo.ca | Sarah Richardson Design custom furniture: Scoop Dining Chairs and Cole Counter Stools, sarahrichardsondesign.com | Tonic Living: dining chair fabric (Victoria Fog), pillow fabric (Majorca Cotton Smoke and Iona Channel Velvet Blue Smoke), tonicliving.ca | Caesarstone: Pure White 1141 counter top, caesarstone.ca | Around the Block: vase on counter, vintage pottery on open shelf, aroundtheblock.com | Client's own: vase on dining table and artwork | Smeg: toaster, smeg.com | Circa Lighting: Dot Stance 13" Rotating Pendant, circalighting.com | C.C. Leathers Inc.: Benchmark Pebble Leather on counter stools, contractleathers.com | Elte Mkt: accessories on open shelf, eltemkt.com | Y & Co.: pillow fabric (Clay Mclaurin Brush No. C07), ycocarpet.com | Tasco Appliances: Dacor range hood and stove, tascoappliance.ca | Fisher & Paykel: dishwasher, fisherpaykel.com | Benjamin Moore: Horizon OC-53 wall paint, Chantilly Lace OC-65 perimeter cabinetry paint, and Wolf Gray 2127-40 peninsula cabinetry paint, benjaminmoore.com.

LIVING ROOM: Vintage: coffee table | Sarah Richardson Design custom furniture: Cory Sofa, Victoria Chair, Lolita Chaise, sarahrichardsondesign.com | Regal Fabrics: sofa fabric (Othello Vanilla), regalfabrics.com | Sarah Richardson Design for Kravet: chair fabric (Zig and Zag Silver), sarahrichardsondesign.com | Sarah Richardson for Palliser: Vista Round Side Table, sarahrichardson.palliser.com | Regina Andrew: Gear Alabaster Table Lamp, Quatrefoil Alabaster Table Lamp Large, reginaandrew.com | Hopson Grace: Bash Vessel small and large bowls, hopsongrace.com | Around the Block: candlesticks, glass table accessories, brass accessories, and white box, aroundtheblock.com | Client's own: clock, artwork, and fireplace insert | Tonic Living: pillow fabric (Meadow Cotton Pebble, Iona Channel Velvet Blue Smoke), chaise fabric (Sunday, Inside Out Velvet, Ivory), tonicliving.ca | Putti Fine Furnishings: floor lamp, putti.ca | World's Away: Harrington Side Table, worlds-away.com | Bungalow 5: Audrey Cabinet and Edward Lounge Chair, bungalow5.com | Kravet: pillow fabric (Dash Off Quartz, Building Blocks Truffle), kravet.com | Elte Mkt: Constantine Natural/Grey Rug, eltemkt.com | Eli Barr: artwork on mantle, artwork above cabinet, instagram.com/ebarr56 | PPG Paints: Antique White 40YY 83/043 wall paint, ppgpaints.com.

GUEST LOUNGE: Tonic Living: drapery fabric (Capri Cotton Mist) and pillow fabric (Valentina Velvet Mineral), tonicliving.ca | Canadian Drapery Hardware: drapery hardware, cdhltd .com | Kathy Richardson Photography: artwork, kathyrichardsonphotography.ca | Indigo: frames, chapters.indigo.ca | DiNuovo Granite & Marble: end table marble fabrication, dinuovo .ca | Regina Andrew: Joan Alabaster Table Lamp, reginaandrew.com | Dash & Albert: Tansy Blue Woven Rug, annieselke.com | Sarah Richardson Design custom furniture: Cory Love Seat, sarahrichardsondesign.com | Vintage: Hex tables | Around the Block: vase, aroundtheblock.com | Y & Co.: pillow fabric (Clay Mclaurin Brush No. C07), ycocarpet.com | Benjamin Moore: Cotton Balls OC-122 wall paint, benjaminmoore.com.

GUEST BEDROOM: Elte Mtk: rug | World's Away: Valentina White Dresser, worlds-away.com | Renwil: mirror, renwil.com | Circa Lighting: Loire Small Sconce, circalighting.com | Tonic Living: drapery fabric (Capri Cotton Mist), headboard fabric (Valentina Velvet Mineral), and pillow fabric (Mason Velvet Lakeland Blue), tonicliving .ca | Canadian Drapery Hardware: drapery hardware, cdhltd.com | Sarah Richardson Design custom furniture: Allison Headboard and rails, sarahrichardsondesign.com | Penney & Co.: green bottles, penneyandcompanyhome.com | Jong Young Flower Market: white/gold vase, jongyoungflowermarket.ca | CB2: boxes, cb2.ca | Benjamin Moore: Cotton Balls OC-122 wall paint, benjaminmoore.com.

GUEST BATHROOM: Circa Lighting: Chirac Small Sconce, circalighting.com | Lavish Kitchens + Fine Cabinetry: vanity, lavishkitchens.ca | Wayfair: Luz Lucite & Satin Brass Bar Knobs and mirror, wayfair.ca | TAPS Bath: Rubinet Hexis Series sink, faucet, towel bar, shower system, tub, tapsbath .com | Home Sense: towels, homesense .ca | Saltillo: 12" x 24" Statuario and 3/8" x 3/8" Moonstone floor tiles, 2" x 8" White Subway & Statuario Pencil wall tiles, saltillo-tiles .com | Around the Block: various glass accessories, aroundtheblock.com | Ciot: Cipollino Bluette countertops, ciot.com | West Elm: modern shower curtain rings, westelm.ca | Benjamin Moore: Paper White OC-55 wall paint and Smoke Gray 2120-40 cabinetry paint, benjaminmoore.com.

PRINCIPAL BEDROOM: Worlds Away: Marcus Gray Nightstand, worlds-away.com | Arteriors: Albany Lamp, arteriorshome.com | Dash & Albert: Layers Hooked Wool Rug, annieselke.com | Sarah Richardson Design custom furniture: Colen Headboard, sarahrichardsondesign.com | Regal Fabrics: headboard fabric (R-Renley Cream), regalfabrics.com | The Bay: bedding, thebay.com | Canvas Gallery: Joe Yunfeng Zhao artwork, canvasgallery.ca | Kravet: pillow fabric (Plein Air Quartz and Baturi Mist) and drapery fabric (Branches Sand), kravet.com | Benjamin Moore: Paper White OC-55 wall paint, benjaminmoore.com.

PRINCIPAL BATHROOM: TAPS Bath: Axor Montreaux Shower System, Axor Montreaux Faucet, Axor Montreaux wallbar and shower kit,

tapsbath.com | Saltillo: Chevron Cararra, 2" x 8" White Bevel Subway and Cararra Pencil shower tiles; Big Square Calcatta floor tiles, saltillo-tiles.com | Sunshade: Hunter Douglas shade (002007 white/pearl), sunshade blinds .com | Wayfair: Rathburn Mirror and Purist Wall Mounted Towel Ring, wayfair.ca | Circa Lighting: Orbel Wall Sconce, circalighting.com | Lavish Kitchens + Fine Cabinetry: vanity, lavishkitchens .ca | Lowe's: Richelieu Rectangular Knob, lowes .ca | Home Sense: towels, homesense.ca | Ciot: Calcatta countertop, ciot.com | Para Paints: Coin Silver P2146-04 cabinetry colour, para.com | Benjamin Moore: White Wisp OC-5 wall paint, benjaminmoore.com.

DAUGHTER'S BEDROOM: Dash & Albert: Tala Woven Jute Rug, annieselke.com | Tonic Living: drapery fabric (Ida Embroidered Sheer), tonicliving.ca | Canadian Drapery Hardware: drapery hardware, cdhltd.com | Sarah Richardson for Palliser: Shore Terrace Bench in Cream and Stripe Denim Throw Blanket, sarahrichardson .palliser.com | IKEA: bed, ikea.com | The Bay: bedding, thebay.com | Worlds Away: Garbo Cerused Oak Nightstand, worlds-away .com | Regina Andrew: Bimini Table Lamp, reginaandrew.com | Canvas Gallery: artwork, canvasgallery.ca | Kravet: pillow fabrics (Spot on Blanc and Mona Zebra Flaxseed), kravet.com | Glidden: Natural white 50YY 83/029 wall paint, glidden.com.

BASEMENT BATH: Saltillo: 12" x 24" Sky Blue Honed floor tiles, saltillo-tiles.com | CB2: Octagon Mirror, cb2.ca | Circa Lighting: Oxford 18" Bath Sconce, circalighting.com | Lavish Kitchens + Fine Cabinetry: vanity, lavishkitchens.ca | Lowe's: Richelieu Round Knob, lowes.ca | TAPS Bath: Kohler Vertical Sink, Rubinet Genesis Faucet, Rubinet T22GNLCHCH Shower Kit, tapsbath .com | Wayfair: Elegant 4-Piece Bathroom Hardware Set, wayfair.ca | Ciot: Donna Grey countertop, ciot.com | Benjamin Moore: Vanilla Milkshake 2141-70 wall paint, Decorator's White CC-20 cabinetry paint, benjaminmoore.com.

"BEACHHOUSE BLUES," pages 40 to 59
GENERAL: Architect: Brooks & Falotico, brooksandfalotico.com | Builder: Thomas and Lord, thomasandlord.com | Stylist: Frances Bailey, francesbailey.com.

KITCHEN: The Urban Electric Company: pendants, urbanelectric.com | Serena & Lily: stools, serenaandlily.com | Heritage Tile: subway tiles, heritagetile.com | Benjamin Moore: Stratton Blue HC-142 island paint, Wythe Blue HC-143 pendant paint, benjaminmoore.com.

EXTERIOR: Northeast Lantern: sconces, northeastlantern.com | Benjamin Moore: Wythe Blue HC-143 door paint, benjaminmoore.com.

DINING ROOM: The Urban Electric Company: pendants, urbanelectric.com | RH: table, rh.com | Palacek: chairs, palacek.com.

LIVING ROOM (both views): Thayer Design Studio: rug, thayerdesignstudio.com | Hickory Chair: sofa, hickorychair.com | Lee Industries: ottoman, leeindustries.com | Delany and Long: ottoman fabric, delanyandlong.com | Serena & Lily: floor lamps, serenaandlily.com | Oomph Home: coffee table, oomphhome.com.

PRINCIPAL BEDROOM: Lekker Home: chair, lekkerhome.com.

PRINCIPAL BATHROOM: Maine Art Hill: Ellen Welch Granter painting, maine-art.com | Benjamin Moore: Pale Smoke 1583 vanity paint, benjaminmoore.com.

DAUGHTER'S ROOM: Blu Dot: pendant, bludot.com | Ballard Designs: chair, quilt, pink lamp, ballarddesigns.com | Radish Moon: floral pillow fabric, radishmoon.com | RH Teen: mirror, rhteen.com | Chelsea Textiles: bureau, chelseatextiles.com | Oomph Home: headboard, oomphhome.com.

BLUE GUEST ROOM: The London Factory: headboard, thelondonfactory.com | Les Indiennes: quilt, lesindiennes.com | Schoolhouse: lamp, schoolhouse.com.

KIDS' BUNKROOM: RH: bedding, rh.com | Marset: sconce, marset.com.

SCREENED-IN PORCH: Northeast Lantern: sconces, northeastlantern.com | Kingsley Bate: sofa, table, kingsleybate .com | Christopher Farr: pillow fabric, christopherfarr.com.

"COLOUR THEORY," pages 60 to 67
GENERAL: Construction Management: Cliff & Evans, cliffandevans.com | Moncer: flooring throughout, moncer.com | Classic Mouldings: plaster frieze, classicmouldings.com | Farrow & Ball: Studio Green 93 wall paint, Pitch Black 256 trim paint, farrow-ball.com | Benjamin Moore: Dolphin AF-715 frieze and ceiling paint, benjaminmoore.com.

CONFERENCE AREA: Kelly Wearstler: Groundworks Jubilee wallpaper, kellywearstler.com | Robert James: table, robertjamescollection.com | Kravet: chairs, GP & J Baker upholstery fabric, kravet.com | Apparatus Studio: pendant, apparatusstudio.com | Studio Marta Manente: swing, martamanente.com.br/en.

KITCHEN: Ciot: marble counter, ciot.com | GP & J Baker: Nympheus Teal wallpaper, kravet.com | ADH hardware: hardware, adhhardware.com | Oggetto: Seagrass Lampshade, oggetto.com | Bilbrough & Co.: floor runner, bilbroughs.com | Farrow & Ball: Bancha 298 cabinet paint, farrow-ball.com.

LIBRARY/GILLIAN'S OFFICE: ADH hardware: hardware, adhhardware.com | Schumacher: wallpaper inset, wallpaper behind desk, fschumacher.com | Gillian Gillies Interiors: desk, gilliangillies.com | CB2: desk chair, cb2.com | Farrow & Ball: Bancha 298 shelf paint, farrow-ball.com.

BATHROOM: Nina Campbell: Peony Place wallpaper, ninacampbell.com | Ciot: marble counter, ciot.com | Kallista: sink, kallista.com | Kohler: faucet, kohler.com | Kravet: wall sconce, kravet.com | Farrow & Ball: Bumble Bee wallpaper, Pitch Black 256 trim and millwork paint, farrow-ball.com.

GALLERY WALL: Gillian Gillies Interiors: daybed, gilliangillies .com | Kelly Wearstler: pillow fabric, kravet.com | Schumacher: fringe trim, fschumacher.com.

"RANCH REVIVAL," pages 82 to 97
GENERAL: First Class Flooring: engineered floors, firstclassflooring.ca | Invisirail: glass railing system, invisirail.com | Glidden: White On White 30GY 88/014 wall paint, glidden.com.

LIVING ROOM: Sarah Richardson for Palliser: Boulevard Tall Salon Table, Boulevard Zinc Round Mirror, Courtyard Quilted Rectangle Ottoman, Summit Charcoal Rug, Hopscotch Stone Pillow, sarahrichardson.palliser.com | IKEA: FÄRLÖV Sofabed in flodafors white, VEDBO Armchair in gunnared dark grey, STOCKHOLM footstool in delikat white and black, YPPERLIG LED floor lamp in dark grey, picture frames, ikea .com | Permanent Press Editions: Brenda fine art flower print, permanentpresseditions.com | Hopson Grace: Treeware wood candlesticks, hopsongrace.com | DiNuovo Granite & Marble: marble fabrication, dinuovo.ca | West Elm: Foundations Metal Footed Vases, westelm.com | Wayfair: grey swirl pillow, wayfair .ca | Pottery Barn: charcoal pillow, potterybarn.com | Provide: Martha Sturdy resin tray, providehome.com | Elte Mkt: round bowl, eltemkt.com | Shutterstock: black and white grass print, shutterstock.com | Electisaurus: vase on side table, eclectisaurus.com.

KITCHEN: IKEA: VOXTORP Cabinets in dark grey, NYMÅNE Pendant Lamp, VIMMERN Kitchen Faucet, LUFTMASSA/ HEMMA Pendant (made into wall sconces), sink, ikea.com | Saltillo: Nordic Grey floor tiles, saltillo-tiles.com | Caesarstone: Pure White 1141 counter top, caesarstone.ca | DiNuovo Granite & Marble: marble fabrication, dinuovo.ca | Dawn Ray: pot lights, dawnray.ca | Home Depot: backsplash tile, homedepot .ca | KitchenAid: stove, vent hood, refrigerator, dishwasher, kitchenaid.ca | Article.: Anco White Counter Stool, article .com | Vintage Fine Objects: rectangle wooden cutting boards, vintagefineobjects.com | Indigo: round wooden cutting boards, chapters.indigo.ca | Sarah Richardson Design: tea towel, sarahrichardsondesign.com | Eclectisaurus: vintage bowl, eclectisaurus.com | Around the Block: vintage grey round bowls, aroundtheblock.com | Hopson Grace: white platters, hopsongrace.com | Jong Young Flower Market: large clear vase, jongyoungflowermarket.ca | Nespresso: Vertuo Next Machine, Bianco Forte Coffee Capsules, nespresso.com.

DINING ROOM: IKEA: VOXTORP cabinets for credenza, MÖCKELBY Table, OFANTLIGT Bowls, FORMIDABEL Plates, BRUNSTA/HEMMA Pendant Lamp, ikea.com | Article.: Dot Dining Chair, article.com | Caesarstone: Pure White 1141 on credenza, caesarstone.ca | ALESSI: silver tray, alessi.com | Walmart: glassware, walmart.ca | White Orchid Prints: art prints, etsy.com | Crate & Barrel: art frames, crateandbarrel .com | Real Canadian Superstore: marble accessory on credenza, realcanadiansuperstore.ca | Around the Block: crystal candlesticks, aroundtheblock.com | West Elm: black and white stripe boxes, white oval bowl, westelm.com | Wayfair: wall sconces, wayfair.ca | Benjamin Moore: Gray 2121-10 table leg paint, benjaminmoore.com.

PRINCIPAL BEDROOM: Sarah Richardson for Palliser: Shore End Tables, Shore Floor Mirror, sarahrichardson.palliser.com | IKEA: SNEFJORD Bed Frame, EVEDAL Pendant Lamp, LEJONGAP curtains (drapery and Roman blind fabrication), TJILLEVIPS Rattan Basket, OFELIA VASS Duvet Cover Set, ikea.com | Brewster Home Fashions: Caro Eggshell Polka Dots wallpaper (sku: 379040), brewsterwallcovering.com | Tonic Living: fabric (Olivia Natural), tonicliving.ca | Kravet: velvet pillow fabric, kravet.com | Renwil: round mirror, renwil.com | Indigo: gallery picture frames, chapters.indigo.ca | Minted: Rolling Vines and Tomah art prints, minted.com | Aero Studio: alarm clock, aerostudios.com | Around the Block: vintage footed bowl, aroundtheblock.com.

PRINCIPAL BATHROOM: The Rubinet Faucet Company: GENESIS Series lavatory faucet and shower system, rubinet .com | IKEA: GODMORGON 24" Vanity Cabinets, ikea.com | Saltillo: SP 4" x 8" Grey Ceramic backsplash tiles, NT Panal 6" x 7" 967 Porcelain floor tiles, saltillo-tiles.com | Circa Lighting:

Beckham Modern Double Sconce, Tob by Thomas O'Brien, circalighting.com | Ciot: marble slabs, ciot.com | DiNuovo Granite & Marble: marble fabrication, dinuovo.ca | True North Glass Co.: shower glass installation, tngc.ca | Renwil: mirror, renwil.com | Home Depot: sink, homedepot.ca | Real Canadian Superstore: towels, realcanadiansuperstore.ca | CB2: Hex Polished Nickel Knobs, cb2.ca | Elgin Picture & Frame: art frame, elginpictureandframe.com | Around the Block: vintage glass bowl, aroundtheblock.com.

GUEST BEDROOM: Sarah Richardson for Palliser: Robin's Palette Rug, Doodle Seaspray Accent Pillow, sarahrichardson.palliser.com | IKEA: VÄXJÖ Pendant Lamp, NYMÅNE Light, LANGESUND Mirror, LURÖY Slatted Bed Base, TIBAST Curtains in white, MAUSUND Natural Latex Mattress, SEKTION Wall Cabinets, VEDDINGE Cabinet Doors, boxspring, bed sheets, ikea.com | Brewster Home Fashions: Tia Blue Texture wallpaper (sku: 2821-25139), brewsterwallcovering.com | Kravet: Lee Jofa fabric (Marie Print Leaf), kravet.com | Macy's: quilted duvet cover set, macys.com | Around the Block: vintage green vases, aroundtheblock.com.

MAIN BATHROOM: The Rubinet Faucet Company: R10 Series lavatory faucet and shower system, rubinet.com | IKEA: ROTSUND Mirror, GODMORGON 48" and 24" Vanity Cabinets, SEKTION 30" x 40" Wall Cabinets, VEDDINGE Cabinet Doors, ikea.com | Saltillo: Carrara 12" x 24" Honed floor tiles, Carrara 10" x 50" Stacked Polished shower floor tiles, saltillo-tiles.com | Caesarstone: Pure White 1141 on tub deck, caesarstone.ca | Ciot: marble slabs, ciot.com | DiNuovo Granite & Marble: marble fabrication, dinuovo.ca | Invisirail: shower glass, invisirail.com | True North Glass Co.: shower glass and hardware installation, tngc.ca | Wayfair: Kaeden 1-Light Armed Sconce, wayfair.ca | Home Depot: American Standard toilet, homedepot.ca | Real Canadian Superstore: waste basket, towels, realcanadiansuperstore.ca | CB2: 3" Brushed Brass Bin Pull, cb2.ca.

KIDS' BUNKROOM: Sarah Richardson for Palliser: Polka Denim 20" x 20" Accent Pillow, Runway Denim 20" x 20" Accent Pillow, sarahrichardson.palliser.com | IKEA: BUSKBO Armchair, NYMÅNE Light, ROTSUND Mirror, HAUGSVÄR Hybrid Mattress, VEDDINGE Cabinet Doors, BERGPALM Duvet Cover and Pillowcase(s), ikea.com | Brewster Home Fashions: Hoppet Grey Folk wallpaper (sku: WV1454), brewsterwallcovering.com | Kravet: Roman blind fabric (Kravet Basics sku: 35531-1), kravet.com | Miller Island: vintage vanity console and stools, millerislandcompany.com | Wayfair: rug, table lamp (shade painted grey), wayfair.ca | Para Paint: Gondolas Of Venice P5155-51 slotwall/bunk bed paint, para.com | PPG Paints: Barley Beige 30YY 68/024 trim paint, ppgpaints.com.

BASEMENT BATHROOM: The Rubinet Faucet Company: H20 Series faucet and shower system, rubinet.com | IKEA: VOXTORP Storage Cabinets in light beige, ikea.com | Saltillo: shower and floor tiles, saltillo-tiles.com | True North Glass

Co.: shower glass, tngc.ca | Ciot: vanity marble, ciot.com | DiNuovo Granite & Marble: marble fabrication, dinuovo.ca | Renwil: mirror, renwil.com | Kohler: sink, kohler.ca | Elte Mkt: white bowls, eltemkt.com | Real Canadian Superstore: towel, realcanadiansuperstore.ca | American Standard: toilet, americanstandard.ca.

MEDIA ROOM: Sarah Richardson for Palliser: Annex Duplex Cocktail Table, Facet Cloud Rug, Hopscotch Stone Throw, Laneway Charcoal Throw, Vista Round End Table, Boulevard Arch Chair, Avenue Chair, sarahrichardson.palliser.com | IKEA: NYMÅNE Pendant Lamp, SKÄGGÖRT Cushion Cover, VEDBO Armchair, SANDANE Mirror, MORABO Sectional, vase, ikea.com | Invisirail: glass railing system, invisirail.com | Arteriors: sconce, arteriorshome.com | Wayfair: round side table, rug, wayfair.ca | Ciot: remnant marble, ciot.com | DiNuovo Granite & Marble: marble fabrication, dinuovo.ca | Napoleon: fireplace insert, napoleon.com | YJInteriors: The Trapezoid Gold Brass Mirror Steel Table Legs (for ping-pong table), etsy.com | Vintage: brass floor lamps | Kravet: accent pillow fabrics, kravet.com | Jong Young Flower Market: round wicker object, jongyoungflowermarket.ca.

"CLASSIC ON THE CAPE," pages 98 to 115
GENERAL: Architect/Builder: Polhemus Savery DaSilva, psdab.com.

LIVING ROOM: Lisa Tharp Collection: swivel chairs, ottoman, sectional, daybed, lisatharp.com/collection | Lisa Tharp for Ecos: fireplace paint, Fluting, ecospaints.net | Visual Comfort: picture light, visualcomfort.com | The Urban Electric Company: pendant, urbanelectric.com.

DINING ROOM: Lisa Tharp Collection: table, lisatharp.com/collection | Lisa Tharp for Ecos: door paint, Chatham Door, ecospaints.net | The Urban Electric Company: pendant, urbanelectric.com | Baldwin Hardware: door hardware, baldwinhardware.com.

PRINCIPAL BEDROOM: Lisa Tharp Collection: chair, folding screen, ottoman, bedside table, lisatharp.com/collection | Copper Lantern Lighting: pendant, copperlanternlighting.com | Arteriors: table lamp, arteriorshome.com | Merida Studio: rug, meridastudio.com | Sara MacCulloch: artwork, sarahmacculloch.com.

TWIN BEDROOM: Design No. 5: wallpaper, fabric, designnofive.com | Visual Comfort: sconce, visualcomfort.com.

GUEST BEDROOM: Visual Comfort: sconce, visualcomfort.com | Bungalow 5: table, bungalow5.com | Cory Silken: photograph, corysilken.com.

"TUDOR TWIST," pages 116 to 131
GENERAL: Builder: Kevin Cradock, cradockbuilders.com.

SITTING ROOM: Cisco Brothers: chairs, ciscohome.net | Holly Hunt: chair fabric, hollyhunt.com | Wisteria: Moroccan table, wisteria.com.

KITCHEN: The Galley: sink, **thegalley.com** | Brizo: faucets, **brizo .com** | Wolf: induction range, **subzero-wolf.com** | Sun Valley Bronze: hardware, **sunvalleybronze.com**.

DINING ROOM: Kevin Cradock: table, **cradockbuilders.com** | Roll & Hill: pendant, **rollandhill.com** | B&B Italia: chairs, **bebitalia.com** | Lawson Fenning: buffet, **lawsonfenning.com** | William McLure: artwork, **williammclure.com**.

LIVING ROOM: Arteriors: bar cart, **arteriors.com** | Verellen: chair, **verellen.biz**.

POWDER ROOM: RH: sink, **rh.com** | Waterworks: faucet, **waterworks.com** | Zak+Fox: wallpaper, **zakandfox.com**.

PRINCIPAL BEDROOM: Fortuny: pendant, **fortuny.com** | Brunschwig & Fils: floral pillow fabric, **kravet.com** | Charles H. Beckley: bedframe, **chbeckley.com**.

PRINCIPAL BATHROOM: Farrow & Ball: Peony wallpaper, **farrow-ball.com**.

"ALPINE FARMHOUSE," pages 132 to 149
GENERAL: Field Design: architect, Steve Sopinka, **fieldesign.ca** | Ed Leimgardt Contracting: builder, **edleimgardtcontracting .com** | Sunshade: Hunter Douglas shades (002007 white/pearl), **sunshade-blinds.com** | Northern Wide Plank: New Haven Plank, Wixom Collection flooring, **northernwideplank.ca** | Ashburne Designs: millwork, **ashburnedesigns.com** | Glidden: White On White 30GY 88/014 wall paint, **glidden.com**.

LIVING ROOM: EQ3: Cello 3-Piece Sectional with Backless Chaise, **eq3.com** | Artefacts Salvage & Design: coffee table base, **artefacts.ca** | DiNuovo Granite & Marble: marble fabrication, **dinuovo.ca** | Caesarstone: coffee table top, **caesarstone.ca** | Design Within Reach: AJ Floor Lamp, **dwr .com** | Sarah Richardson for Palliser: Trilogy Cashmere Rug, **shopsarahstyle.com** | Lagom 142: throw, **lagom142.com** | Kravet: Kelly Wearstler pillow fabrics, **kravet.com** | Y & Co: Peter Dunham Pillow, **ycocarpet.com** | Tonic Living: lumbar pillow fabric, **toniclivng.ca**.

NOOK: Design Within Reach: Tolomeo Wall Lamp, **dwr.com** | Sipa: tree table, Vienna chairs, **sipasedie.it** | Kravet: bench cushion and lumbar pillow fabrics, **kravet.com** | Y & Co: Peter Dunham pillows, **ycocarpet.com**.

DESK AREA: Turquoise Palace: Stockholm Lounge Chair, **turquoisepalace.com** | Sarah Richardson for Palliser: Boulevard Tall Salon Table, Courtyard Round Small Ottoman, **sarahrichardson.palliser.com** | Kravet: Christopher Farr pillow fabric, **kravet.com**.

FIREPLACE: DiNuovo Granite & Marble: marble fabrication, **dinuovo.ca** | Ciot: Pina Colada marble, **ciot.com** | Sarah Richardson for Palliser: Courtyard Round Small Ottoman, Trilogy Cashmere Rug, **shopsarahstyle.com** | Design Within Reach: chair, ottoman, **dwr.com** | EQ3: Prana Basket, **eq3.com** | Holly Ann Friesen: artwork, **buttergallery.ca** | Renaissance Rumford: fireplace insert, **renaissancefireplaces.com**.

MUSIC AREA: Sarah Richardson for Palliser: Courtyard Round Small Ottoman, **sarahrichardson.palliser.com** | Gabriella

Collier: artwork, **buttergallery.ca** | Project Turntable: Record Player, **project-audio.ca**.

KITCHEN: DiNuovo Granite & Marble: marble fabrication, **dinuovo.ca** | Caesarstone: Pure White 1141 counter top, **caesarstone.ca** | Ciot: Arabescato marble backsplash, **ciot.com** | TAPS Bath: Blanco Rondo sink, Grohe Minta Pull Out Faucet, Blanco 10 U 1-½ island sink, **tapsbath.com** | Tasco Appliances: Wolf Pro 36" 6 Burner Range, **tascoappliance.ca** | Article: stools, **article.com** | Ridgely Studio Works: Aura Slim Pendant, **ridgelystudioworks.com**.

DINING ROOM: Design Within Reach: pendants, About a Chair 22 Armchair, **dwr.com** | Artefacts Salvage & Design: dining table and console table, **artefacts.ca** | Sarah Richardson for Palliser: Stride Swivel Chair, Boulevard Tall Salon Table, Laneway Charcoal Throw, **sarahrichardson.palliser.com** | EQ3: Solid Teak Round Stool, **eq3.com** | Kravet: Kelly Wearstler pillow fabric, **kravet.com**.

PRINCIPAL BEDROOM: Arteriors Home: Mia Pendant, **arteriorshome.com** | Sarah Richardson for Palliser: Collage Natural Rug, **shopsarahstyle.com** | Suzanne McNenly: artwork, **buttergallery.ca** | Tonic Living: pillow fabric, **toniclivng.ca** | Design Within Reach: Parallel Bed, Louis Poulsen sconces, **dwr .com** | Kravet: Kelly Wearstler bench and pillow fabric, **kravet .com** | Lagom 142: baskets, **lagom142.com** | EQ3: Prana basket, **eq3.com**.

PRINCIPAL BATHROOM: Rich Brilliant Willing: Crisp Sconce, **rbw.com** | DiNuovo Granite & Marble: marble fabrication, **dinuovo.ca** | Wayfair: sink, **wayfair.ca** | TAPS Bath: Rubinet Genesis Wide Spread Faucet, **tapsbath.com** | Saltillo Tiles: shower walls, shower floor, and main floor tiles, **saltillo-tiles .com** | True North Glass Co: Mirror and shower glass, **tngc .ca** | Ciot: Breccia Capraia shower wall, **ciot.com** | Lagom 142: Baskets, **lagom142.com** | Home Sense: towels, **homesense.ca**.

STAIRS: Invisirail: glass railing system, **invisirail.com**.

MAIN BATHROOM: Rich Brilliant Willing: Hoist Sconce, **rbw.com** | DiNuovo Granite & Marble: marble fabrication, **dinuovo.ca** | Wayfair: Verticyl Sink, **wayfair.ca** | TAPS Bath: Rubinet Genesis Wide Spread Faucet, **tapsbath.com** | Vintage: vases | Saltillo: shower and main floor tiles, **saltillo-tiles .com** | True North Glass Co: mirror and shower glass, **tngc.ca** | Ciot: Iceberg Blue countertops, **ciot.com**.

BLUE/GREEN BEDROOM: EQ3: Cello Bed in Mila Silver, **eq3.com** | Sarah Richardson for Palliser: Boulevard Tall Salon Table, **sarahrichardson.palliser.com** | IKEA: wall lamp, duvet, **ikea.com** | Kravet: pillow fabric, **kravet.com** | Butter Gallery: artwork, **buttergallery.ca** | Lagom 142: throw blanket, **lagom142.com**.

PINK BEDROOM: EQ3: Cello Bed in Mila Silver, **eq3.com** | IKEA: nightstand, table lamp, duvet, **ikea.com** | Bilbrough: pillow fabric, **bilbroughs.com** | Lagom 142: throw blanket, **lagom142.com**.

MUDROOM: Ed Leimgardt Contracting: bench, **edleimgardtcontracting.com** | Lagom 142: basket, hooks, **lagom142.com**.